The Big Book of Fun Things to Do in Retirement

Kick-Start Your New Adventure Today! Hundreds of Exciting and Unconventional Ideas for a Fabulously Happy Retirement

D1715286

Joseph Hufschmitt

The Big Book of Fun Things to Do in Retirement: Kick-Start Your New Adventure Today! Hundreds of Exciting and Unconventional Ideas for a Fabulously Happy Retirement

Contents

Dear Reader,

I hope you find great value in this book. I pulled together many diverse and unusual ideas into this one source to save you time. If you find this to be a helpful resource, please consider leaving a review on Amazon. It is very helpful to others who are searching for this type of information and helps a small, independent author such as myself.

Thank you,

Joseph Hufschmitt

Here is a QR code link to the review page on Amazon.com (U.S. site).

Introduction

"You are never too old to set a new goal or dream a new dream."

—C.S. Lewis

People have lots of different ideas about retirement, but I assume you have this book because you want to make sure you have all the ideas. I attempted not to leave any out.

I think you will agree that you have never heard of or imagined many of these topics, but this list is also grounded in suggestions that may have crossed your mind. The variety and number are breathtaking. You will want to explore this vast smorgasbord so you can pick the best for yourself. But I must warn you, some of these are hilarious or have humorous components. So, if you laugh unexpectedly, rest assured we will get back down to business shortly.

Whatever you want to do, you now get to choose. If you want to sit on the couch and watch *Gunsmoke* and *Perry Mason* reruns, you can do that. You have the time. But if you get fidgety and want to tackle something more challenging, you can do that also.

I included ideas for men and women, old and young. Though I am in the U.S., I attempted to present lots of ideas that apply to anyone on the globe. Though retirement happens for most later in life, it can happen earlier if you are financially able. Therefore, some of the suggestions might appeal to younger retirees but may be out of reach to those much older.

I assume there are readers spanning a broad range of abilities and limitations. I am not constraining my audience to some notion of a stereotypical retiree. This book contains suggestions that are appropriate for those with no limitations on their mental and physical abilities as well as lots of ideas for people in the middle and for those that are very limited. I leave it up to you to decide what appeals to you.

1

You are unique. Embrace what you can do, and please consider it sheer entertainment to laugh at suggestions that are "so not you." You can have fun imagining what a debacle it would be for you to attempt those activities that are beyond your reach.

Retirement gives you two treasures that you should guard with every fiber of your being—more free time and less stress. Now, I know I may get pushback from you about stress. All of us have different situations, whether it is finances, family responsibilities, or health. But at least the stress associated with the job you worked for so many years is behind you.

Take some time to think about what is really important to you. Time is passing quickly, and it is precious. A year from now, you should be able to look back and feel really satisfied that you got a tremendous amount of fulfillment out of that time. You should be able to identify what you did and get a big smile on your face. You absolutely do not want to look back and wonder where the time went and what you did with it. Decide right now that you are resolved to put meaning in your life every day and that you have a goal and milestones.

Even if it is just to enjoy family and spend your time with them, create a list of what you want out of it. Perhaps journal each day so you can look back and remember each dinner, each visit, and what was memorable, pleasant, and worthwhile about that day.

This book is not just a bunch of things to do with your time. It is an array of doorways to fulfillment. You get to peek behind each of them to decide what hidden surprise might be exciting to you and bring you the most happiness for your time.

About This Book

Some ideas in this book are presented with a fair amount of detail, but many ideas are described more briefly. All of them are just starting points. If something catches your fancy, type it into Google or YouTube or get a book specific on the topic to delve deeper. The goal here is to let you know these things exist.

You can reinvent yourself. Now that you are free from your daily job commitment, you may want to create a new career for yourself. Perhaps there is a passion you have always wanted to pursue. If you are healthy enough and think clearly enough, this is the perfect opportunity to launch into something you enjoy. My caution is to make sure it is something you really enjoy, something that is not going to create stress.

There are online training opportunities as well as many local opportunities for training. So, if what you want to do requires learning a skill, start there. Think ahead about what you will do with that skill. Will you still be able to manage your time as you want? Will it be easy to take the day to go to the doctor if you need to?

My point is, if you decide you have always loved to cook and you train to become a chef, you may get locked into a job where you can't take time off anytime you please. Instead, consider joining a cooking club so that you can maintain control over your schedule while also having a forum for expressing your passion for cooking. So, if your passion is leading you to something to make money, ask yourself if you are trading your freedoms. Is this going to lock you into a certain location? Is this going to lock you into a certain schedule? Is this going to introduce stress into your life? If the answer to any of these questions is yes, then alarm bells should be going off in your head. "Danger, Will Robinson! Danger!" (Taking a reference from the TV series *Lost in Space*.)

Chapter 1
A Sample of This and That

"Stay young at heart, kind in spirit, and enjoy retirement living."

—Danielle Duckery

Dance Walking

Incorporate dance into your daily walks by adding music and rhythm to your steps. Dance walking combines cardiovascular exercise with the joy of dance, boosting mood and energy levels. It is a unique and entertaining form of exercise that combines the health benefits of walking with the joy and expression of dance.

Dance walking involves walking to the rhythm of music while incorporating dance movements into your steps. It's a fun and energetic way to get your body moving and your heart pumping.

Start by selecting music with a lively beat and a tempo that motivates you to move. You can choose your favorite songs or create a playlist specifically for dance walking.

Begin your dance walking session with a gentle warm-up to prepare your body for movement. Perform some light stretching exercises to loosen up your muscles and joints.

Once you're warmed up, begin walking at a comfortable pace. Focus on maintaining good posture and utilizing your core muscles as you walk.

As you walk, start incorporating simple dance moves into your steps. This can include movements like side steps, kicks, twists, hip shakes, arm swings, and toe taps. Let the music inspire you, and move your body in whatever way feels natural.

Pay attention to your surroundings, and make sure you're walking in a safe environment, free from obstacles or hazards. Stay aware of traffic if you're walking outdoors.

The most important aspect of dance walking is to have fun and enjoy yourself! Don't be self-conscious. Immerse yourself in the music and movement.

Once you've completed your dance walking session, take some time to cool down and stretch your muscles again. This will help prevent stiffness and reduce the risk of injury.

Dance walking offers numerous health benefits, including improved cardiovascular fitness, increased calorie burn, enhanced coordination, and mood-boosting effects. It's also a great way to relieve stress and boost your overall sense of well-being.

One of the best things about dance walking is that it's highly customizable and adaptable to your preferences. You can mix and match different dance moves, styles of music, and walking routes to keep things interesting and exciting.

Overall, dance walking is a fun and accessible form of exercise that anyone can enjoy, regardless of age or fitness level. So, put on your favorite tunes, lace up your walking shoes, and start dancing your way to better health and happiness!

Fermentation Workshops

Take part in fermentation workshops where you learn to ferment foods such as sauerkraut, kimchi, kombucha, yogurt, kefir, and sourdough bread. Fermentation promotes gut health, digestion, and immune function. Fermentation workshops are educational events where participants learn about the ancient art and science of fermentation.

The workshop usually begins with an overview of fermentation, explaining the basic principles and processes involved. Participants learn about the role of microorganisms, such as bacteria and yeast, in fermenting various foods and beverages.

The instructor may discuss the health benefits of fermented foods and drinks, highlighting their probiotic properties, nutrient content, and potential impact on gut health and digestion.

Safety guidelines for fermentation are typically covered to ensure participants understand how to ferment foods safely and avoid potential risks, such as contamination or spoilage.

Participants are often given the opportunity for hands-on learning, with demonstrations on how to ferment different foods and beverages.

Information is provided about the ingredients and equipment needed for fermentation, including fermentation vessels, starter cultures, salt, sugar, water, and various flavorings and seasonings.

Common issues and troubleshooting tips are discussed, such as how to identify and prevent mold growth, how to control fermentation temperature, and how to adjust fermentation times for desired results.

Participants often have the opportunity to taste a variety of fermented food and beverages and experience the diverse flavors and textures that fermentation can produce.

There is usually time set aside for questions and answers, allowing participants to seek clarification on any aspects of fermentation they're curious about or may not fully understand.

Participants may receive handouts, recipes, or instructional guides to take home, providing them with reference materials and resources for continuing their fermentation journey.

Fermentation workshops often foster a sense of community among participants who share a common interest in fermentation. It's an opportunity to connect with like-minded individuals, share experiences, and learn from each other.

Overall, fermentation workshops offer a fun and educational experience where participants can learn valuable skills for fermenting their own foods and beverages at home. Whether you're a beginner looking to dip your toes into fermentation or an experienced fermenter looking to expand your knowledge, there's something for everyone to gain from attending a fermentation workshop.

Competitive Beard Growing

Join beard-growing competitions and events where participants compete to grow the longest, most creative, or most elaborate beards. Embrace the camaraderie of fellow beard enthusiasts, and showcase your facial hair prowess.

Competitive beard growing, also known as beard competitions or beard contests, is a unique and increasingly popular event where participants showcase their facial hair in various categories to compete for prizes, recognition, and bragging rights.

Beard competitions often feature multiple categories based on factors such as length, style, thickness, and overall appearance of the facial hair. Common categories include:

- Longest Beard: Participants compete to grow the longest beard, measured from the chin to the tip of the longest hair.
- Full Beard: This category includes all styles of full beards, from natural to styled, with participants judged on factors like density, shape, and grooming.
- Partial Beard: Participants with facial hair styles such as goatees, sideburns, or mustaches compete in this category.
- Styled Beard: This category focuses on creative and artistic beard styles, including elaborate designs, braids, twists, and sculpted shapes.
- Whiskerina: A category specifically for women or individuals who don't have facial hair but create and wear fake beards made from materials like yarn, fabric, or hair extensions.

Participants typically register for the competition in advance, either online or in person, and pay an entry fee. They may also need to provide information about their beard, including its length, style, and any special grooming or styling techniques used.

Competitors are judged by a panel of judges based on specific criteria relevant to each category. Judging criteria may include factors such as length, thickness, density, symmetry, overall appearance, creativity, and grooming.

Competitors spend weeks or months growing and grooming their beards in preparation for the competition. This may involve regular trimming, shaping, conditioning, and styling to achieve the desired look.

On the day of the competition, participants gather at a designated venue where the event is held. Each participant takes turns stepping onto the stage or platform to showcase their beard to the judges and audience.

Judges evaluate each participant's beard based on the established criteria and assign scores accordingly. At the end of the competition, winners are announced in each category, and prizes may be awarded for first, second, and third place, as well as special awards for categories like "Best in Show" or "People's Choice."

Beard competitions often foster a sense of camaraderie and community among participants, who share a common interest in facial hair and grooming. Competitors may bond over their shared experiences, exchange tips and advice, and support each other throughout the event.

Many beard competitions are held as fundraising events for charitable causes or nonprofit organizations. Participants and spectators may be encouraged to donate to support a worthy cause, adding an element of philanthropy to the event.

Overall, competitive beard growing is not just about facial hair; it's also about creativity, craftsmanship, and camaraderie. Whether you're a seasoned competitor or a curious spectator, beard competitions offer a fun and entertaining experience for all involved.

Extreme Ironing

Combine the boring with the exciting by trying extreme ironing. Iron laundry in unusual and adventurous locations such as on mountainsides, in caves, while skydiving, while skiing, in water, or even underwater! Extreme ironing was started in 1997 in Leicester, England. All you need to get started is an iron, a board, and some clothes. With enough dedication, you may make it to the world championships.

Haunted Doll Adoption Agency

This is a possible side business that might be fun. Create a business offering haunted doll adoption services where customers can adopt allegedly haunted dolls with mysterious histories and paranormal activity. Provide adoption certificates and storytelling sessions about each doll's past.

A haunted doll adoption agency is a fictional or themed establishment that presents itself as a place where individuals can adopt haunted or possessed dolls. While these agencies are often part of the paranormal entertainment industry and are not genuine, they serve as a creative and immersive experience for those interested in the supernatural or horror genre.

Presentation is an important factor. Haunted doll adoption agencies may have physical locations, websites, or social media platforms where they present their collection of haunted dolls. They often use eerie or spooky aesthetics to create a mysterious and intriguing atmosphere.

Each haunted doll is accompanied by a backstory or description that details its alleged haunted history, including information about its previous owners, mysterious occurrences, and paranormal activities associated with the doll.

Interested individuals can browse the selection of haunted dolls and choose one to adopt. The adoption process may involve filling out a form, providing personal information, and agreeing to certain terms and conditions.

Haunted doll adoption agencies may charge an adoption fee for each doll, which can vary depending on factors such as the doll's rarity, condition, and perceived level of haunting or possession.

Once the adoption is finalized, the haunted doll is typically shipped to the adopter's address. Shipping and handling fees may apply, and the doll may be packaged in a special or themed manner to enhance the experience.

Adopters may receive documentation or certificates of adoption for their haunted dolls, adding to the authenticity and immersive nature of the experience.

Haunted doll adoption agencies often foster a sense of community among adopters by providing forums, social media groups, or events where individuals can share their experiences, stories, and photographs of their haunted dolls.

While haunted doll adoption agencies are primarily for entertainment purposes, they also serve as a platform for storytelling and creative expression within the paranormal genre. The stories and descriptions associated with each haunted doll contribute to the overall narrative and atmosphere of the experience.

Some haunted doll adoption agencies offer customization options, allowing adopters to request specific features or characteristics for their haunted dolls, such as personalized names, backstories, or haunting experiences.

Haunted doll adoption agencies typically include disclaimers or warnings to remind adopters that the haunting or possession associated with the dolls is fictional and for entertainment purposes only. They may also provide safety tips or guidelines for interacting with the dolls.

Overall, haunted doll adoption agencies provide a unique and immersive experience for individuals interested in the paranormal or horror genre, allowing them to explore the supernatural world through storytelling, creativity, and entertainment. Whether you believe in haunted dolls or not, these agencies offer an intriguing and captivating way to engage with the supernatural realm.

Community Theaters

Get involved in community theater productions by volunteering as an actor, stagehand, usher, or set builder. Volunteering in community theaters offers a vibrant and rewarding experience for individuals who are passionate about the arts and enjoy being part of a creative community.

Community theaters rely heavily on volunteers to fill a variety of roles both onstage and offstage. Volunteers may participate as actors, directors, stage managers, set designers, costume designers, makeup artists, lighting technicians, sound engineers, ushers, ticket sellers, and more.

One of the most visible roles in community theater is acting. Volunteers can audition for roles in upcoming productions and work closely with directors and fellow actors to bring characters to life on stage.

Behind the scenes, volunteers work on the production team to bring the vision of the director to fruition. This may involve building sets, creating costumes, designing lighting and sound effects, and ensuring that all technical aspects of the production run smoothly.

Stage managers play a crucial role in coordinating rehearsals and performances, managing the backstage crew, and ensuring that actors are ready and in their places when needed.

Volunteers can assist with front-of-house duties, such as greeting patrons, selling tickets, handing out programs, and ushering audience members to their seats.

Volunteers with skills in marketing, graphic design, or social media can help promote upcoming productions and events, reaching out to the community through advertising, press releases, and online platforms.

Community theaters often rely on fundraising efforts to support their operations. Volunteers can help organize fundraising events, seek out sponsors and donors, and apply for grants to secure funding for future productions.

Some community theaters offer educational programs and outreach initiatives for youth and underserved communities. Volunteers can assist with teaching workshops, organizing youth productions, or bringing theater into schools and community centers.

Volunteering in community theaters provides opportunities to collaborate with fellow theater enthusiasts, build connections within the local arts community, and expand your network of contacts in the industry.

In addition to contributing to the success of the theater, volunteering offers personal growth and development opportunities. Volunteers can learn new skills, gain experience in various aspects of theater production, and develop confidence and self-expression through creative endeavors.

Overall, volunteering in community theaters is a fulfilling way to support the arts, engage with your community, and be part of a dynamic and collaborative artistic endeavor. Whether you're a seasoned theater professional or someone with a passion for the arts, there are countless ways to get involved and make a meaningful contribution to your local theater community.

Create a Bucket List of Destinations

If you've always wanted to travel, now is the time. Here are some bucket list destinations that you might find particularly enticing.

Explore the ancient ruins of Machu Picchu in Peru. It is a UNESCO World Heritage Site nestled in the Andes Mountains. Marvel at the breathtaking scenery and rich history of the Inca civilization.

Visit Santorini, Greece. Experience the iconic beauty of Santorini's whitewashed buildings, stunning sunsets, and crystal-clear waters. Immerse yourself in the laid-back island lifestyle of this idyllic Greek destination.

Wander through the romantic canals and charming alleyways of Venice, Italy. Known for its historic architecture, world-class art museums, and delicious cuisine, experience the magic of this unique city on water. While you're in Italy, you may also want to explore the picturesque villages and stunning views of the Amalfi Coast. You can soak up the Mediterranean sun, savor delicious seafood and pasta dishes, and wander through charming streets lined with colorful houses and lemon groves.

Discover the traditional culture and serene beauty of Kyoto, Japan. It is home to ancient temples, lush bamboo forests, and stunning cherry blossoms. Immerse yourself in the rich traditions of Japanese tea ceremonies and kimono-clad geisha.

Dive into the vibrant underwater world of the Great Barrier Reef in Australia. It is one of the world's most iconic natural wonders. Snorkel among colorful coral reefs, tropical fish, and marine life.

Embark on a once-in-a-lifetime safari adventure in the Serengeti National Park in Tanzania. You can witness the awe-inspiring spectacle of the annual wildebeest migration and spot the Big Five (lion, elephant, buffalo, leopard, and rhinoceros) in their natural habitat. Another safari destination is Kruger National Park, South Africa. It is one of Africa's largest game reserves where you may also spot the Big Five as well as a wide variety of other wildlife species.

Experience the otherworldly beauty of the Northern Lights in Iceland, where you can marvel at the dancing colors of the Aurora Borealis against the backdrop of snow-capped mountains and icy landscapes.

Discover the unique wildlife and pristine natural beauty of the Galapagos Islands of Ecuador. They are home to giant tortoises, marine iguanas, and blue-footed boobies. Explore the volcanic landscapes and crystal-clear waters of this remote archipelago.

Embark on a road trip adventure through New Zealand's South Island, where you can explore dramatic fjords, pristine beaches, and snow-capped mountains, and experience adrenaline-pumping activities like bungee jumping, skydiving, and heli-skiing, which involves taking a helicopter to access remote areas and slopes of virgin powder snow.

Stand in awe of the vastness and beauty of the Grand Canyon in the USA. This is one of the world's most iconic natural wonders. Hike along the rim or raft down the Colorado River for an unforgettable outdoor adventure.

Marvel at the architectural masterpiece of the Taj Mahal in India. It is a symbol of love and devotion. Explore the rich history and culture of India's vibrant cities, ancient temples, and bustling markets.

Embark on an expedition cruise to Antarctica, Earth's last frontier, where you can witness towering icebergs, majestic glaciers, and incredible wildlife, such as penguins, seals, and whales, in their natural habitat.

Get away to Bora Bora, French Polynesia. Relax in luxury on the pristine beaches of Bora Bora, surrounded by crystal-clear lagoons, overwater bungalows, and lush tropical scenery. Indulge in water sports, spa treatments, and romantic sunsets.

Walk along the ancient ramparts of the Great Wall of China, one of the most impressive architectural feats in history. Marvel at the breathtaking views of the surrounding mountains and countryside.

Experience the awe-inspiring power and beauty of Iguazu Falls. It is a collection of stunning waterfalls that straddle the border between Argentina and Brazil. Explore the lush rainforest ecosystem that surrounds them.

Soar high above the otherworldly landscapes of Cappadocia, Turkey in a hot air balloon. Marvel at the surreal rock formations, fairy chimneys, and ancient cave dwellings that dot the landscape below.

Discover the ancient temples and ruins of Angkor Wat in Cambodia. It is one of the most important archaeological sites in Southeast Asia. Marvel at the intricate carvings, towering spires, and grandeur of this UNESCO World Heritage Site.

Trek through the rugged wilderness of Patagonia, which lies in both Chile and Argentina. You can explore dramatic landscapes, towering peaks, and crystal-clear lakes, and embark on adventures such as hiking, horseback riding, and glacier trekking.

These bucket list destinations offer the opportunity for unforgettable travel adventures. You can experience new cultures and create lasting memories that will be cherished for years to come. Whether you're seeking adventure, relaxation, or cultural enrichment, there's a destination out there that's perfect.

Chapter 2
Start a Hobby

"Retirement gives you the time, literally, to recreate yourself through a sport, game, or hobby that you always wanted to try or that you haven't done in years."

—Steven Price

Photography

Starting a photography hobby can be an exciting and rewarding journey. My own photography journey started as a boy with a Kodak Brownie Starflash camera. I can remember being with my mom and dropping off my film to be developed at the Photo Bug booth in the parking lot of the grocery store.

In later years, I had various instant cameras and film cameras, but I was never very devoted to the hobby. After a few decades, I developed a desire to dive deeper into photography. So, I purchased a film SLR (single lens reflex) camera, lenses, tripod, and flash. I knew nothing, but I got a book and started learning how it worked. I loved my 100mm macro lens for taking very close-up pictures of single crabapple blossoms and other flowers. I also loved my wide-angle lens for pulling vast scenes into a single frame. Being able to switch lenses on a camera greatly expands your creative options for capturing an image.

Eventually, I got a DSLR. That's a digital single lens reflex camera. I will never look back at film. Things have only gotten better over the years. Fortunately, most of the lenses I originally purchased continued to fit the newer camera bodies I purchased. This is something to keep in mind. If you get a camera with interchangeable lenses, you will probably spend more on the lenses than on the camera.

My point to this personal side trip is that my interests ebb and flow, and the money I spent was appropriate for my level of interest at the time. You may need to try the hobby out for a while to decide if it really holds your interest before you start investing too much money.

Here's a guide to help you get started.

Start out by defining your interests. Determine what aspect of photography interests you the most. Do you enjoy capturing landscapes, portraits, wildlife, street scenes, small details, or something else? Understanding your interests will help you focus your efforts in selecting equipment and finding resources that improve your skills in that area.

Choosing the right camera and lenses can make a big difference in your results. Anyone just starting would want to start with a digital camera. Film is still used by some photographers for artistic and other reasons, but with the current great digital technology, this is where you want to be. Digital cameras offer immediate feedback and flexibility.

Consider factors such as budget, size, weight, and features when choosing a camera. Entry-level DSLRs, or mirrorless cameras, are great options for beginners and offer a good balance of performance and affordability.

Also, it is astonishing how good smartphone cameras have become. Some higher-end phones have incredible camera controls and settings. You may find you have all the creative control you need with the camera in your smartphone. If nothing else, it is an easy, inexpensive starting point. You can do a lot more with a phone than just taking a selfie at a restaurant.

Learn the basics. Familiarize yourself with the fundamental concepts of photography, including exposure, composition, aperture, shutter speed, ISO, and white balance. Understanding these concepts will lay a solid foundation for your photography journey.

Explore online resources, photography books, tutorials, and courses to learn about the technical aspects of photography and how to use your camera effectively. There are many YouTube content creators that provide a wealth of knowledge.

Practice regularly. The key to improving your photography skills is practice. Make a habit of taking your camera with you whenever you go somewhere, and capture images regularly. Review your results on your computer or other large screen. You will find that they seem very different from the small screen on the back of your camera. You will also start to develop your eye. This will be especially true when you follow the work of professional photographers.

Experiment with different settings, compositions, lighting conditions, and subjects to expand your skills and creativity. Don't be afraid to make mistakes, because they are valuable learning opportunities.

Study various composition techniques, such as the rule of thirds, leading lines, framing, symmetry, and perspective. Understanding composition will help you create visually appealing and engaging images.

Analyze the work of renowned photographers, and study how they use composition to tell stories and evoke emotions in their images. To analyze your favorite photographer's work, you may want to search to see if they have published articles about their style and technique. There may also be interviews where they explain what went into creating some of their images. These stories can be fascinating and eye-opening. Some of the National Geographic photographers have produced amazing work and have amazing stories.

Experiment with editing software. Familiarize yourself with photo editing software, such as Adobe Lightroom, Photoshop, or free alternatives like GIMP or Snapseed. Editing allows you to enhance your images, correct exposure and color balance, and unleash your creativity. Start with basic editing techniques, such as adjusting exposure, contrast, saturation, and cropping. As you gain more experience, you can explore more advanced editing techniques.

Seek feedback and critique. Share your photos with friends, family, or online photography communities to receive constructive feedback and critique. Feedback from others can help you identify areas for improvement and gain new perspectives on your work. Often, you don't know what you don't know. Feedback can help you see things that did not even occur to you.

Join photography clubs, forums, or social media groups where you can connect with other photographers, share your experiences, and learn from each other. A community is a great way to have social interaction.

Build your portfolio. As you continue to practice and improve, curate your best images to build a portfolio that showcases your work. Your portfolio can be digital (e.g., website, online portfolio) or physical (e.g., printed portfolio, photo book). Choose images that demonstrate your unique style, creativity, and technical skills. If you decide to turn photography into a side business, a strong portfolio will help you showcase your talent and attract potential clients or opportunities in the future.

Set goals and keep learning. Set specific, achievable goals for your photography journey, whether it's mastering a new technique, capturing a particular subject, or participating in a photography competition. Stay curious, and never stop learning. Photography is a vast and ever-evolving field, so continue to explore new techniques, experiment with different styles, and seek inspiration from the work of other photographers.

By following these steps and staying dedicated to your photography hobby, you'll gradually develop your skills, expand your creative vision, and derive immense joy and satisfaction from capturing the world through your lens.

Create a Collection

Retirement is a great time to start a collection. For many, the enjoyment comes from the hunt. Each collectible has its own peculiar way of hiding in this world. Your pursuit may take you into many interesting places, whether physically or online. The enjoyment of these new places, and the sometimes unbelievable stories of a series of convoluted events that led to finding each item in your collection, creates a series of memories you recall every time you gaze upon your collection.

Some collections require very little money while others can be quite expensive. Some require quite a bit of space while others are very compact. For example, collecting cars is going to be much more expensive and take a lot more space than collecting postcards. Some collections may require you to travel great distances while others can be done online. Also, consider how much actual joy you will derive from the collection and the pursuit. If you are the obsessive type, consider whether this is something you can control once you start. Think of how many times you have seen a news article where someone collected pets, then when they were finally rescued from themselves, they had 70 pets running around their house.

Here is a list to get your creative juices flowing.

Delve into the world of antiques and collect items such as furniture, pottery, glassware, or decorative objects from different historical periods.

Start a coin collection focusing on coins from different countries, historical periods, or specific denominations. An added perk is you get the new title of numismatist.

Collect stamps from around the world, focusing on different themes, countries, or rare and unique stamps. Then, you can call yourself a philatelist.

Build a collection of postcards from your travels or from different regions, featuring scenic views, landmarks, or historical sites.

Rediscover the toys of your childhood or collect vintage toys from different eras, such as action figures, dolls, board games, or model trains.

Explore the world of vinyl records, and collect albums from your favorite artists or genres, or seek out rare and collectible records.

Dive into the world of comic books, and collect issues from different publishers, characters, or story arcs.

Collect sports memorabilia such as autographed items, jerseys, trading cards, or equipment from your favorite sports teams or athletes.

Build a library of books on a specific topic, genre, or author, or collect rare and first-edition books for your personal collection.

Start a collection of art prints, focusing on different artists, styles, or periods of art history.

Create a collection of miniatures, such as dolls, figurines, or model vehicles, buildings, or landscapes.

Explore the world of photography by collecting vintage cameras from different manufacturers, eras, or styles.

Start a collection of teapots, focusing on different shapes, sizes, materials, or designs.

Collect antique or vintage maps, atlases, or globes from different regions or historical periods.

Build a collection of vintage or novelty kitchen gadgets, such as egg beaters, can openers, or cookie cutters.

Start a collection of keychains from different places you've visited or featuring different themes, characters, or designs.

Collect corkscrews from around the world featuring different designs, materials, or mechanisms.

Collect movie memorabilia, such as posters, props, or costumes, from your favorite films or genres.

Build a collection of seashells from your travels to different beaches or coastal regions, focusing on different shapes, colors, or species.

Start a collection of matchbooks from restaurants, hotels, or businesses you've visited, or seek out vintage or rare matchbooks for your collection.

Here is an expanded treatment of a collection option that can take up as much or as little space as you want, can be very expensive or relatively inexpensive, and you can either travel quite a bit or do most of it online:

Collecting Hello Kitty items can be a delightful and whimsical hobby that brings joy and nostalgia. Hello Kitty merchandise comes in a wide variety of items, including plush toys, figurines, clothing, stationery, kitchenware, accessories, and more. You can explore different categories and choose the ones that resonate with you the most. I have a Hello Kitty switch plate in my office, and it is very cheery. I also have a six-inch Hello Kitty plushy that stares at me from its perch in a mug on the corner of my desk. I find it a rather soothing companion and much easier to care for than a real cat. I am somewhat artistic, so I play the "A" card if anyone tries to give me any grief. I feel like I can cross many boundaries with impunity.

Hello Kitty items often feature different themes and collaborations, such as seasonal collections, movie tie-ins, or collaborations with other brands. You can focus on collecting items from specific themes or collaborations that interest you.

Many cities around the world have Hello Kitty themed cafés, stores, and attractions where fans can immerse themselves in the world of Hello Kitty. You can plan visits to these locations as part of your collecting adventures. I visited a Hello Kitty store in the Miami, Florida, area, and it was amazing to see.

Hello Kitty conventions and events are held regularly, where fans can buy, sell, and trade Hello Kitty merchandise, meet other collectors, and participate in themed activities and workshops. You can attend these events to expand your collection and connect with fellow fans.

Joining online communities and forums dedicated to Hello Kitty collectors can be a great way for you to connect with other fans, share your collections, and exchange tips and advice on collecting.

You can take pleasure in displaying your Hello Kitty collection in your home, whether it's setting up a dedicated display shelf, curating themed vignettes, or incorporating Hello Kitty items into your décor.

If you enjoy hands-on activities, you can add an extra layer of creativity to your collecting hobby with DIY and crafting projects related to Hello Kitty. You can create custom items, refurbish vintage pieces, or even design your own Hello Kitty-inspired creations.

Hello Kitty items can make delightful gifts for family and friends, especially for younger generations that may also appreciate the timeless charm of Hello Kitty. You can enjoy sharing your passion for collecting by giving thoughtful gifts from your collection.

Keeping track of your collection by documenting and cataloging items can add a sense of organization and accomplishment to the hobby. You can create digital or physical catalogs, take photos of your collection, or keep detailed records of your acquisitions.

Hello Kitty collectors often organize meetups and swap meets where members can meet in person, trade items, and share their love for Hello Kitty. You can participate in these gatherings to connect with other collectors and expand your collection through trades and swaps.

Overall, collecting Hello Kitty items can be a fun and rewarding hobby that allows you to indulge in nostalgia, express your creativity, and connect with a vibrant community of fans. Whether it's hunting for rare treasures, attending themed events, or simply enjoying the adorable charm of Hello Kitty, there's something for every collector to enjoy in the world of Hello Kitty.

In conclusion, these are just a few ideas for fun collections to create. Whether you're interested in history, art, pop culture, or hobbies, there's a wide range of collectibles to explore and enjoy. Collecting can be a rewarding and enjoyable hobby that allows you to express your interests, learn new things, and connect with others who share your passion.

Tombstone Rubbing

Tombstone rubbing is a unique and fascinating hobby that involves creating reproductions of inscriptions and designs found on gravestones.

To get started with tombstone rubbing, you'll need some basic materials, including soft paper or fabric (such as rice paper or muslin), charcoal or graphite sticks, masking tape, and a clipboard or similar firm surface.

Visit cemeteries with old or historically significant gravestones that feature interesting inscriptions, designs, or textures. Be respectful of the graves, and avoid damaging fragile or weathered stones.

Clean the surface of the gravestone with a soft brush or cloth to remove dirt, debris, and vegetation. Use masking tape to secure the paper or fabric firmly against the stone, ensuring it lies flat and smooth.

Hold the charcoal or graphite stick at a slight angle and gently rub it across the surface of the paper or fabric, following the contours of the inscription or design on the gravestone. Apply even pressure to create a clear and detailed reproduction.

Experiment with different rubbing techniques to achieve the desired effect. You can vary the pressure, angle, and speed of the rubbing to capture fine details, textures, and shading.

Pay attention to the intricate details and nuances of the gravestone, such as lettering styles, decorative motifs, and symbols. Take your time to ensure that you're rubbing accurately and capturing these elements.

Once you've completed the rubbing, carefully remove it from the gravestone. If you picked up any moisture from the stone, allow the paper to dry completely. You can further preserve the rubbing by spraying it with a fixative or applying a thin layer of archival wax.

Record relevant information about the gravestone, such as the name of the deceased, dates of birth and death, and any other inscriptions or symbols. This information can help contextualize your rubbing and contribute to its historical significance.

Consider framing your tombstone rubbings or mounting them on archival backing for display in your home or as part of a collection. Store them in a cool, dry place away from direct sunlight to prevent fading or damage over time.

Always approach tombstone rubbing with respect and sensitivity for the gravesites and the families of the deceased. Obtain permission from cemetery authorities before engaging in rubbing activities, and avoid causing any harm or disruption to the gravestones or surrounding areas.

Tombstone rubbing can be a meaningful and educational hobby that allows enthusiasts to explore local history, art, and culture while preserving the legacy of those who have passed away. By creating reproductions of gravestone inscriptions and designs, tombstone rubbers contribute to the documentation and appreciation of our shared heritage.

Electric Trains

The electric train hobby, also known as model railroading or model trains, is a popular pastime enjoyed by enthusiasts of all ages. It involves the construction, operation, and display of miniature trains and landscapes.

Model trains come in various scales, which represent the size of the models compared to real trains, and gauges, which represent the distance between the rails. Common scales include HO scale (1:87), N scale (1:160), O scale (1:48), and G scale (1:22.5). Each scale has its own advantages and considerations, such as space requirements and level of detail.

Hobbyists typically set up a layout, which is a miniature representation of a railroad system, complete with tracks, scenery, buildings, and landscaping. Layouts can be simple or elaborate, and they can be built on tables, shelves, or dedicated platforms. Some enthusiasts create permanent layouts in basements or spare rooms, while others build modular layouts that can be assembled and disassembled for shows and exhibitions.

Model trains run on tracks, which are typically made of metal rails mounted on plastic or wooden ties. The tracks are powered by electricity, either through a direct current (DC) system or an alternating current (AC) system. Trains are equipped with electric motors that draw power from the tracks to propel them forward and backward. Hobbyists can choose from a wide variety of locomotives, passenger cars, freight cars, and other rolling stock to create their own custom trains.

Model trains can be controlled manually, using handheld controllers, or electronically, using digital command control (DCC) systems. DCC systems allow hobbyists to operate multiple trains independently on the same track, control the speed and direction of each train individually, and program advanced features such as sound effects, lighting, and animation.

Creating realistic scenery and landscaping is an important aspect of the electric train hobby. Hobbyists use a variety of materials, such as foam, plaster, paper, and paint, to model terrain features such as mountains, rivers, forests, and fields. They also add details such as buildings, bridges, roads, vehicles, and people to bring their layouts to life.

Many hobbyists enjoy building and customizing their own models from kits or scratch-building parts from raw materials. They may also modify and combine existing models, in a process known as kitbashing, to create unique and personalized trains and structures.

Operating model trains requires skill and attention to detail. Hobbyists must carefully monitor the performance of their trains, maintain the tracks and electrical systems, and troubleshoot any problems that arise. Regular cleaning and lubrication are essential to keep trains running smoothly and prevent damage to delicate components.

Model railroading is a social hobby, and enthusiasts often join clubs, attend shows, and participate in exhibitions to share their passion with others. Clubs provide opportunities for networking, learning, and collaboration while shows and exhibitions allow hobbyists to display their layouts to the public and admire the work of others.

Overall, the electric train hobby offers a rich and rewarding experience for enthusiasts who enjoy creativity, craftsmanship, and the nostalgia of railroads. Whether you're a beginner or an experienced modeler, there's always something new to learn and explore in the world of model trains.

I got an electric train as a Christmas present when I was a kid and loved it for many years. Of course, my sister and I did kid things with it, like put our pet hamsters in the coal cars, run the train into little plastic blocks to derail the train, and pretend like the cows had escaped from the livestock freight cars. No hamsters were ever actually harmed, and it was immense fun. I think back to the *Addams Family* episodes where Gomez would blow up the bridge as his electric train was passing over. Perhaps these are a little extreme for adults, but they highlight the immersive fun you can have as you gaze on your train passing through the little world you've created.

Shooting

The shooting hobby, also known as shooting sports or recreational shooting, involves the safe and responsible use of firearms for sport, competition, or leisure. It encompasses a variety of disciplines and activities, each with its own rules, equipment, and techniques. I know for some this may be a bit controversial, and it may pertain more to those in the USA. My wife had never been shooting, so I took her to a range. After carefully reviewing safe handling as well as wearing hearing and eye protection, I gave her a large caliber semi-automatic handgun to try out. She fired it downrange, and then the biggest smile stretched across her face. She absolutely loved it. It was exhilarating and loud. She had so much fun that day as she blew through several boxes of ammunition. So, if you've never tried it, you might be very surprised by how much fun you have.

There are several types of shooting disciplines within the hobby.

Target shooting involves aiming at stationary or moving targets, often at fixed distances and with specific shooting positions.

Clay target shooting involves participants shooting at clay targets (clay pigeons) launched into the air from machines.

In competitive shooting, there are organized matches where participants compete against other shooters in various disciplines, such as pistol, rifle, shotgun, or multi-gun competitions.

Hunting involves using firearms to pursue and harvest game animals or birds in their natural habitat. It requires knowledge of wildlife, hunting regulations, and firearm safety.

Participants use different types of firearms depending on the shooting discipline. Common firearms include pistols, revolvers, rifles, shotguns, and air guns (pellet guns). Firearms vary in caliber, action type (semiautomatic, bolt-action, lever action, etc.), and configuration (long guns, handguns, etc.).

Safety is paramount in the shooting hobby. Participants must adhere to strict safety rules and procedures to prevent accidents and ensure a safe shooting environment. This includes proper handling, storage, and maintenance of firearms, as well as following range rules and wearing appropriate safety gear (ear and eye protection).

Many shooting enthusiasts undergo training and education to improve their shooting skills, learn firearm safety protocols, and understand local laws and regulations. This may involve formal training courses, workshops, or self-study using books, videos, and online resources.

In addition to firearms, shooters use various equipment and accessories to enhance their shooting experience and performance. This may include ammunition, targets, shooting stands or benches, shooting bags or rests, cleaning kits, and specialized gear for competitive shooting (such as holsters, magazine pouches, or shooting vests).

Shooting enthusiasts typically practice and compete at shooting ranges or facilities specifically designed for shooting sports. These facilities may include indoor or outdoor ranges, skeet and trap fields, rifle ranges, and hunting preserves. Some shooting ranges offer rental firearms and instruction for beginners.

The shooting hobby has a vibrant community of enthusiasts who share a passion for firearms, marksmanship, and shooting sports. Participants often join clubs, associations, or shooting organizations to connect with like-minded individuals, participate in events and competitions, and advocate for the preservation of Second Amendment rights.

The shooting hobby offers many benefits, including physical exercise, stress relief, mental focus, and personal satisfaction from improving shooting skills and achieving goals. It also fosters camaraderie, sportsmanship, and respect for firearms and their safe and responsible use.

Overall, the shooting hobby provides a challenging and rewarding recreational pursuit for individuals interested in firearms, marksmanship, and shooting sports. Whether for competition, hunting, or leisure, the shooting hobby offers opportunities for skill development, social interaction, and outdoor enjoyment.

Building Plastic Models

Building plastic models, often referred to as scale modeling or model making, is a hobby that involves assembling and painting miniature replicas of various objects, such as vehicles, aircraft, ships, buildings, and figures, using plastic model kits.

Plastic model kits come in a wide range of subjects and scales. Here are some of the common categories:

- Aircraft: Airplanes, helicopters, and spacecraft
- Military Vehicles: Tanks, armored vehicles, trucks, and artillery
- Ships: Warships, submarines, sailing vessels, and maritime structures
- Automobiles: Cars, trucks, motorcycles, and racing vehicles
- Figures: Soldiers, civilians, animals, and fantasy characters
- Science Fiction and Fantasy: Spaceships, robots, monsters, and fictional vehicles
- Dioramas: Scenes depicting historical events, landscapes, or fictional scenarios

Model kits typically come as plastic sprues (parts trees) containing individual components that need to be cut, cleaned, and assembled according to the instructions provided. Assembly may involve gluing, snapping, or screwing parts together, as well as sanding, filling, and seam work to achieve smooth seams and precise fits.

Once assembled, models are painted and detailed using various techniques to replicate the appearance of the real-life subject. This may include priming, airbrushing, hand painting, weathering, dry brushing, masking, decals, and applying surface finishes, such as gloss, satin, or matte varnish.

Modelers use a variety of tools and materials to build and customize their models, including:

- Cutting Tools: Hobby knives, sprue cutters, and scissors for cutting parts from sprues and trimming excess material
- Adhesives: Plastic cement, cyanoacrylate (super glue), and epoxy for bonding parts together
- Paints: Acrylic, enamel, and lacquer paints in various colors and finishes for painting models
- Brushes and Airbrushes: Paintbrushes and airbrushes for applying paint and weathering effects
- Accessories: Decals, photo-etched parts, resin upgrades, and aftermarket accessories for adding detail and realism to models

Plastic modeling caters to hobbyists of all skill levels, from beginners to advanced modelers. Beginners may start with simple snap-together kits or easy-to-build subjects, while experienced modelers may tackle complex kits with intricate details and advanced techniques.

Plastic modeling has a vibrant community of enthusiasts who share tips, techniques, and inspiration through forums, social media groups, and modeling clubs. There are also many online resources, books, magazines, and video tutorials available to help modelers improve their skills and learn new techniques.

Completed models can be displayed individually or as part of dioramas at home, in model shows, or at modeling competitions. Model shows and competitions provide opportunities for modelers to showcase their work, receive feedback, and connect with other enthusiasts.

Building plastic models offers many benefits, including relaxation, creativity, problem-solving, attention to detail, historical and technical education, and a sense of accomplishment from completing a project. It's a versatile hobby that appeals to individuals with diverse interests, from history and engineering to art and storytelling.

Overall, the plastic modeling hobby provides a rewarding and enjoyable outlet for creativity and craftsmanship, allowing enthusiasts to express their passion for subjects ranging from history and technology to pop culture and imagination. Whether building for fun, relaxation, or artistic expression, modelers find satisfaction in bringing their favorite subjects to life in miniature form.

I and several of my friends quite enjoyed building models as kids. I built battleships, cars, crazy monsters, and even took parts from different models and combined them to make Frankenstein cars that were quite unique. I would spend hours carefully sanding, gluing, masking them off, painting them, and then applying decals. Of course, they eventually took up too much shelf space for my mom to tolerate, and I was put on notice that a lot of them would have to go.

Battleships especially took up quite a bit of space. So, I could recoup the most shelf space with the fewest sacrifices by poaching this category. My friend was in the same jam with his mom. There was only one obvious solution. We had to glue lots of firecrackers to our battleships and take them, along with our BB guns, back into the woods that were behind our neighborhood. There was a pond situated deep in the woods. We set the battleships on fire, pushed them out into the pond, and began pelting them with our BB guns. We would be picking off gun turrets with our shots while black smoke was rising from the burning styrene plastic. The firecrackers would occasionally explode. It was a glorious battle, but, alas, the flotilla was defeated and sank to the murky depths along with all of their crew.

We never accidentally started a forest fire with our antics. And if it is any consolation to all the tree huggers concerned about the pristine environment that was contaminated by bad little boys, that land is now an upper middle-class subdivision with pristine green lawns and paved streets. There is nothing left of those woods by the housing developers that mowed them down.

In case you're wondering, there is a point to all of this. Model building can be lots of fun. We may have enjoyed their destruction a tiny bit more than their construction, but we got immense satisfaction out of creating clean, authentic-looking models. They just looked cool.

Painting and Drawing

Creating art can be very fun and satisfying. Painting and drawing are creative pursuits that involve expressing oneself through the use of paints, pencils, pens, brushes, and other artistic tools to create visual artworks on paper, canvas, or other surfaces.

There are various types of media used in painting and drawing, each with its own characteristics and techniques.

- Painting: Painting media includes acrylics, oils, watercolors, gouache, and tempera. Each type of paint has unique properties in terms of opacity, drying time, texture, and blending capabilities.
- Drawing: Drawing media includes graphite pencils, colored pencils, charcoal, ink, markers, and pastels. Each medium offers different levels of precision, line quality, and texture.

Artists can choose from a wide range of subjects to paint or draw, including landscapes, portraits, still life, animals, abstract compositions, and fantasy/sci-fi themes. Some artists specialize in a particular subject matter while others explore a variety of themes.

Painting and drawing techniques vary depending on the medium and desired effect.

- Layering: Building up layers of paint or pencil to create depth, dimension, and richness of color
- Blending: Mixing colors or shading tones to achieve smooth transitions and gradients

- Texturing: Adding texture to the surface using techniques such as stippling, cross-hatching, sgraffito, or impasto
- Wet-on-Wet vs. Wet-on-Dry: Painting techniques where wet paint is applied onto wet or dry surfaces, each producing different effects
- Composition: Arranging elements within the artwork to create balance, harmony, focal points, and visual interest

Artists use a variety of tools and materials to create their artworks, including some of these.

- Paintbrushes: Different types of brushes for various techniques, such as flat, round, filbert, fan, and detail brushes
- Palette: A surface for mixing and holding paint colors, which can be a traditional palette, palette paper, or palette tray
- Canvas or Paper: Surfaces for painting or drawing, available in various sizes, textures, and weights
- Erasers and Fixatives: Erasers for correcting mistakes and fixatives for preserving finished drawings
- Drawing Boards and Easels: Supports for holding canvases or paper at a comfortable working angle

Painting and drawing are skills that can be developed through practice, experimentation, and study. Artists may take art classes, workshops, or online courses to learn new techniques and expand their artistic abilities.

Artists find inspiration for their artworks from a variety of sources, including nature, everyday life, imagination, personal experiences, and other artists' works. Keeping a sketchbook or visual journal can help artists capture ideas and develop their creative vision.

Completed artworks can be displayed in galleries, exhibitions, or art shows, or shared online through social media, artist websites, or online portfolios. Many artists also sell their artworks through galleries, art fairs, or online marketplaces.

Painting and drawing can be a source of relaxation, stress relief, and personal fulfillment for artists. Engaging in creative activities allows individuals to express themselves, explore emotions, and find joy in the process of making art.

Overall, painting and drawing offer a rich and rewarding outlet for artistic expression, imagination, and self-discovery. Whether painting for pleasure, personal growth, or professional development, artists find satisfaction in bringing their ideas and visions to life through the creation of visual artworks.

Jigsaw Puzzles

Jigsaw puzzles are a popular and timeless hobby enjoyed by people of all ages. I have loved jigsaw puzzles since I was a kid and continue to put one together every so often. I get a certain little joy reward every time I find two pieces that fit together. And if I find three pieces at once, I am elated. I prefer puzzles that are 1,000 pieces or more. Otherwise, they are finished too quickly.

I love the new ones with their vibrant colors, but I also find it nostalgic to work on older puzzles. My mother-in-law gave me a cache of old Milton Bradley puzzles from the 70s. Some of them hadn't even been opened! There were even 2,000- and 2,500-piece puzzles in the group. These are more challenging because the colors are muted and the resolution is lower than many of today's puzzles.

I have created several cardboard trays with very low rims that allow me to segregate specific colors or patterns and assemble these sections separately from the main puzzle. I can slide them in when the rest of the puzzle is far enough along to snap the section in.

Jigsaw puzzles consist of a picture or image that has been mounted onto a sturdy backing material and then cut into interlocking pieces of various shapes and sizes. The goal of the puzzle hobbyist is to reassemble these pieces to recreate the original image.

Jigsaw puzzles come in a wide range of themes, styles, and difficulty levels to suit different preferences and skill levels. Themes can include landscapes, animals, famous artworks, scenic landmarks, cartoons, and much more. Difficulty levels range from simple puzzles with fewer pieces to complex puzzles with thousands of pieces.

Many people find working on jigsaw puzzles to be a relaxing and meditative activity that helps them unwind, reduce stress, and focus their minds. The repetitive task of sorting and fitting puzzle pieces together can be soothing and calming, providing a welcome break from the hustle and bustle of daily life.

Jigsaw puzzles offer numerous cognitive benefits and serve as a form of mental exercise for the brain. Working on puzzles helps improve problem-solving skills, spatial reasoning, pattern recognition, attention to detail, and hand-eye coordination. It can also stimulate the brain and keep the mind sharp as people age.

Jigsaw puzzles are often enjoyed as a social or family activity, bringing people together to collaborate and bond over a shared hobby. Families may gather around a table to work on a puzzle together, enjoying quality time and conversation as they collaborate to solve the puzzle.

Completing a jigsaw puzzle provides a sense of accomplishment and satisfaction for the puzzle solver. There's a feeling of fulfillment and pride that comes from successfully assembling all the pieces and revealing the complete image, especially for larger or more challenging puzzles.

Some people collect jigsaw puzzles as a hobby and enjoy assembling puzzles featuring unique artwork, designs, or themes. Limited edition puzzles, artist-designed puzzles, and puzzles with special features (such as 3D or glow-in-the-dark effects) are particularly sought after by collectors.

Jigsaw puzzles are relatively accessible and affordable compared to many other hobbies. They can be purchased at various price points, depending on factors such as the size, complexity, and quality of the puzzle. Many puzzles can also be found at thrift stores, garage sales, or swapped with friends, making them an accessible hobby for people of all budgets.

Overall, the hobby of jigsaw puzzles offers a delightful combination of relaxation, mental stimulation, creativity, and social interaction, making it a beloved pastime for countless enthusiasts around the world. Whether you're a casual puzzler or a devoted aficionado, there's something uniquely satisfying about the process of piecing together a jigsaw puzzle and experiencing the joy of completion.

Metal Detecting

Metal detecting is a fascinating and rewarding hobby. I built my first metal detector as a kid using a cigar box for the electronics and a wooden stick to hold the coil. I saw the plans in a book and thought it would be fun. It was fairly crude, but it worked well enough. I got a thrill out of finding pennies in the dirt and was a little disappointed when I dug up a bottle cap. I have purchased a few metal detectors over the years. They get more and more sensitive and specialized. I have found rings, cheap jewelry, toys, coins, property stakes, keys, and assorted junk. You never know what you will turn up. It's an amazing power to be able to locate something you cannot see. And it gets you out in the fresh air and is a fairly portable hobby.

Metal detecting requires a metal detector, a handheld device that emits electromagnetic fields to detect metal objects buried underground. Enthusiasts use various types of metal detectors, ranging from basic models suitable for beginners to advanced detectors with specialized features for experienced detectorists. Other essential gear includes headphones, digging tools (such as a shovel, trowel, or digging knife), a finds pouch or bag to carry discovered items, and optional accessories like a pinpointer for precision locating. I definitely recommend you get a pinpointer and headphones if you decide to try metal detecting. These tools make it a lot more enjoyable because you can isolate the target faster and more accurately.

Metal detecting can be practiced in a variety of locations, including parks, beaches, fields, forests, historical sites, and private properties (with permission from the landowner). Each location offers unique opportunities for discovery, with different types of metal objects and artifacts potentially buried beneath the surface. Some detectorists specialize in specific types of locations, such as beach detecting, relic hunting, or searching for coins and jewelry in parks.

Metal detecting can yield a wide range of finds, including coins, jewelry, rings, watches, keys, buttons, relics, artifacts, and other metal items that were lost or discarded over time. Each find has its own story and historical significance, providing insights into the past and local history. Valuable and rare finds, such as gold coins, antique jewelry, or historical artifacts, are particularly exciting and rewarding for detectorists.

One of the most enjoyable aspects of metal detecting is the thrill of discovery. Every beep or signal from the metal detector represents the possibility of finding something interesting or valuable buried beneath the ground. The excitement of uncovering hidden treasures, the anticipation of each find, and the sense of adventure make metal detecting a thrilling and addictive hobby for enthusiasts.

Metal detecting allows enthusiasts to explore outdoor environments and discover hidden treasures in nature. Whether it's searching for coins in a local park, combing the beach for lost jewelry, or exploring historical sites for relics, detectorists have the opportunity to connect with the outdoors, discover new places, and enjoy the beauty of nature while pursuing their hobby.

Metal detecting provides a form of low-impact exercise and physical activity that can be enjoyable and beneficial for health and fitness. Walking or hiking while swinging the metal detector, bending and digging to recover targets, and carrying equipment and finds all contribute to cardiovascular health, strength, and endurance. Metal detecting is suitable for people of all ages and fitness levels, making it a versatile and accessible hobby for everyone.

Metal detecting fosters a sense of community and camaraderie among enthusiasts. Detectorists often share their finds, stories, and experiences with fellow hobbyists, whether in person at metal detecting club meetings, organized events, or online forums and social media groups. The metal detecting community is known for its supportive and friendly atmosphere, where members encourage and inspire one another in their pursuit of treasure hunting.

Metal detecting offers opportunities for research and historical exploration, as enthusiasts uncover artifacts and objects that provide clues to the past. Many detectorists research the history of their local area, study maps, old photographs, and historical records, and collaborate with historians and archaeologists to learn more about the sites they detect. Responsible detectorists follow ethical guidelines and laws governing metal detecting, respect cultural heritage, and contribute to the preservation and documentation of historical artifacts and sites.

Overall, metal detecting is a fun hobby that combines elements of exploration, discovery, adventure, and outdoor enjoyment. Whether you're searching for lost coins in a park, uncovering relics at a historical site, or exploring the beach for buried treasure, metal detecting offers endless opportunities for excitement, enrichment, and enjoyment for enthusiasts of all ages and backgrounds.

Start a Lapidary Hobby

Starting a lapidary hobby involves the exploration and creation of jewelry, sculptures, and decorative items from raw gemstones and minerals. My dad loved cutting, tumbling, polishing, and mounting stones. He also enjoyed rockhounding. I can remember a family trip to Arkansas where we dug quartz crystals out of the red clay. When we got home, he mounted many of the pieces into necklaces. He even had an ultraviolet light to fluoresce the minerals that were in some rocks.

Start by researching the basics of lapidary arts. Learn about different types of gemstones, minerals, and rocks, as well as the tools, equipment, and techniques used in lapidary work. Books, online resources, tutorials, and classes are valuable sources of information for beginners.

Consider joining a local lapidary club or community where you can connect with other enthusiasts, learn from experienced members, and access shared equipment and facilities. Lapidary clubs often offer workshops, demonstrations, and group activities to support learning and skill development.

Invest in basic lapidary tools and equipment to get started. Essential tools may include a rock saw or slab saw for cutting rough stones into manageable pieces, a grinding wheel or lapidary grinder for shaping and smoothing, and a polishing wheel or tumbler for polishing and finishing stones. Additional tools such as calipers, rulers, and safety gear are also necessary for safe and effective lapidary work.

Choose raw gemstones and minerals to work with based on your interests, preferences, and availability. Visit rock and mineral shops, gem shows, or online retailers to purchase rough stones in various shapes, sizes, and colors. Start with softer, more forgiving stones such as agate, jasper, or quartz before progressing to harder gemstones like sapphire or ruby.

Begin practicing basic lapidary techniques, such as sawing, grinding, shaping, and polishing on small, inexpensive stones to develop your skills and familiarity with the tools and equipment. Experiment with different cutting angles, shapes, and finishes to achieve desired results and enhance the beauty of the stones.

Prioritize safety when working with lapidary tools and equipment. Always wear appropriate safety gear such as safety goggles, gloves, and a dust mask to protect against flying debris, dust, and chemicals. Follow manufacturer's instructions and recommended safety practices for each tool and machine, and work in a well-ventilated area with good lighting.

As you gain confidence and proficiency in basic lapidary techniques, explore more advanced techniques and processes such as faceting, cabochon cutting, inlay work, and carving. Take advantage of workshops, classes, and online tutorials to expand your skills and knowledge in specific areas of lapidary arts.

Lapidary arts offer endless possibilities for creativity and self-expression. Experiment with different designs, patterns, and styles to create unique jewelry pieces, sculptures, and decorative items that reflect your personal aesthetic and artistic vision. Don't be afraid to take risks and explore new ideas in your lapidary work.

Lapidary is a lifelong learning journey that offers opportunities for continuous growth and improvement. Stay curious, open-minded, and receptive to new ideas, techniques, and discoveries in the field of lapidary arts. Share your knowledge and experiences with others, and embrace the joy of creating beauty from raw gemstones and minerals.

Starting a lapidary hobby requires patience, dedication, and a passion for working with gemstones and minerals. By following these steps and immersing yourself in the fascinating world of lapidary arts, you can embark on a fulfilling and rewarding journey of exploration, creativity, and self-discovery.

Coffee Roasting

Coffee roasting involves the process of transforming green coffee beans into aromatic and flavorful roasted coffee beans. I started roasting coffee several years ago to both save money and get better tasting coffee. The coffee definitely tastes better than what I had been getting at the grocery store, but the cost ended up being about equivalent. That is in part due to my preference for better varieties of coffee beans.

The whole thing started innocently enough. A family member at one point in his life had been a barista at Starbucks. He became enticed by one of his friends that had started roasting. So, he bought an inexpensive air roaster and a sample assortment pack of green coffee beans from an online source out of California. He, in turn, gave me little sample packs of his roasted batches and was gushing about how great this coffee was and how grocery store coffee was now beneath his palette and yadda, yadda, yadda.

I brought the samples home and brewed some. We just had a drip coffeemaker, but that is all the family member had. So, I tasted it and found that it was smoother. It did not taste like Starbucks, but it was definitely smoother and had a nice character to the taste.

His goading got to me. It was not an option for me to continue expressing my bad taste by brewing the floor scrapings that pass for coffee on the grocery shelves. So, I got the same deal with the air roaster and sample packs.

I like my coffee dark, just like the beans you see in the espresso machines at Starbucks. So, that is what I was shooting for in my roasting process. The first thing I noticed about roasting to this darkness is the smell. It is similar to burnt popcorn. Oh, no. I just ruined your dream about sipping that sublime cup of coffee. I apologize. Suffer on. It gets a little worse. There is also a lot of fine chaff dust that comes from the roaster. This is definitely something that works better outdoors, but I have roasted indoors close to the exhaust fan over my stove. That works okay, but the house still ends up smelling like burnt popcorn for a day or two. Not ideal. So, I went back to roasting outdoors.

Despite these negatives, I found I liked the coffee well enough to continue. My wife also enjoys the coffee, though she adds so much stuff to it I am not sure she actually tastes the coffee.

I eventually got a small drum roaster, and I continued to hone my roasting technique by monitoring the look of the beans, the smell, the temperature, and the cracking sound the beans make as they get toward the end of the roast.

I now buy 50-pound bags of green coffee beans that last me about five or six months. I have also switched over to using a French press to brew my coffee and find that it brings out the wonderful flavor in a big way. It is very different from what you get in a drip coffeemaker.

The irony is that the coffee-snob family member who got me started down this rabbit hole now has both Keurig and Nespresso machines in his kitchen. One is for him, the other for his wife, and he no longer roasts. He just puts the little pods in his machine and acts like everything is fine.

Okay, I tried the pods, and they are fine. I just find it humorous how people's attitudes change. I never have been able to achieve the Starbucks flavor, but I do end up with very flavorful coffee. My sisters always ask me to bring some of my coffee when I visit. So, they must think it tastes better than what they normally drink. I also enjoy being able to select single-origin beans from almost anywhere in the world. Different plantations grow different varieties of coffee, and they use different methods of drying the beans. These all taste different, and you may find favorites you like. If you love coffee, this might be something that is quite rewarding to you.

Here is how to get started.

The process begins with green coffee beans, which are raw and unroasted. These beans are sourced from various regions around the world and come in different varieties with unique flavor profiles.

To roast coffee at home, you'll need a coffee roaster. There are various types of roasters available, including drum roasters, air roasters, even simple popcorn poppers, or modified ovens for DIY roasting. Each type of roaster has its own advantages and produces slightly different results. As I mentioned, my first roaster was an air roaster. It is similar to an air popper for popcorn. It was only capable of roasting a few ounces of coffee at a time. Once I felt comfortable that this was something I wanted to continue doing, I invested in a small drum roaster that allows me to roast almost two pounds at a time.

The roasting process involves applying heat to the green coffee beans to bring out their flavors and aromas. During roasting, the beans undergo chemical changes, known as the Maillard reaction, and caramelization, which develop their characteristic flavors and colors.

As you roast coffee beans, you'll experiment with different roast profiles to achieve the desired flavor profile. This includes factors such as roast level (light, medium, dark), roast time, temperature, and airflow. Each roast profile will produce different flavors, acidity levels, and body in the finished coffee.

Throughout the roasting process, it's important to closely observe and monitor the beans to ensure they roast evenly and reach the desired level of roast. This involves listening for cracks (first crack and second crack), observing changes in color, and monitoring the aroma of the beans.

After roasting, the beans are cooled rapidly to stop the roasting process and preserve their flavors. This can be done using a dedicated cooling tray or simply by transferring the beans to a metal colander and gently shaking them to remove excess heat. Once cooled, the beans are allowed to rest for a period of time (typically 12 to 24 hours) to allow for degassing and development of flavors.

Once the beans have rested, they can be packaged for storage or consumption. Coffee beans should be stored in airtight containers away from light, heat, and moisture to maintain their freshness and flavor. Many home roasters use resealable bags or mason jars for storing their roasted coffee beans.

The final step in the coffee roasting is to brew and taste your freshly roasted coffee. Home roasters can experiment with different brewing methods, such as pour-over, French press, espresso, or cold brew, to highlight the unique flavors of their roasted beans. Tasting and comparing different roast profiles and coffee origins is part of the fun of the learning process in coffee roasting.

Overall, the coffee roasting hobby offers enthusiasts the opportunity to explore the world of coffee from bean to cup, experiment with different roast profiles, and enjoy the satisfaction of creating delicious coffee at home. With practice and experimentation, home roasters can develop their skills and palate to produce high-quality roasted coffee beans tailored to their personal preferences.

Chapter 3
Craft Ideas

"I enjoy waking up and not having to go to work. So, I do it three or four times a day."

—Gene Perret

Small Craft Ideas

Here are some unique small craft ideas where you can express your creativity:

- **Handmade Greeting Cards**: Create custom greeting cards for birthdays, holidays, and special occasions using cardstock, stamps, stickers, and embellishments.
- **Pressed Flower Art**: Press flowers and foliage from your garden or local parks, and use them to create beautiful botanical art pieces, such as framed arrangements or greeting cards.
- **Polymer Clay Jewelry**: Make unique jewelry pieces using colorful polymer clay, including earrings, necklaces, bracelets, and pendants. Experiment with different shapes, patterns, and techniques.
- **Decoupage Vases**: Decorate plain glass or ceramic vases with decorative paper or fabric using decoupage techniques. Add a protective sealant for a glossy finish.
- **Fabric Scrap Quilting**: Use fabric scraps to create patchwork quilts, pillow covers, table runners, or wall hangings. Experiment with different patterns, colors, and quilting techniques.
- **Hand-Embroidered Tea Towels**: Embellish plain cotton tea towels with hand-embroidered designs, such as flowers, animals, or geometric patterns. They make thoughtful and functional gifts.

- **Beeswax Food Wraps**: Make eco-friendly food wraps using cotton fabric and beeswax. These reusable wraps can be used to cover bowls, wrap sandwiches, or store produce.
- **Macramé Plant Hangers**: Create stylish macramé plant hangers using cotton cord or rope. Hang them indoors or outdoors to display your favorite houseplants in style.
- **Wood Burned Coasters**: Personalize wooden coasters with intricate designs or patterns using a woodburning tool. Seal them with a protective finish for durability.
- **Pressed Herb Candles**: Make homemade candles by embedding pressed herbs or flowers into soy or beeswax. They add a natural and aromatic touch to any room.
- **Silversmithing**: Learn the ancient craft of silversmithing, and create your own jewelry and metalwork pieces. Master techniques such as soldering, shaping, and polishing to craft unique and personalized silver jewelry designs.
- **Wood Whittling**: Discover the art of wood whittling, and create intricate carvings and sculptures from wood. Learn basic whittling techniques and about carving tools and safety practices to unleash your creativity and craftsmanship in retirement.
- **Natural Dyeing**: Explore the art of natural dyeing, and create your own colorful fabrics using plant-based dyes. Experiment with different dye sources, such as flowers, leaves, and roots to achieve vibrant and eco-friendly dye colors.
- **Upcycled Magazine Bowls**: Repurpose old magazines or catalogs by weaving strips of paper into colorful and decorative bowls. Use them to hold keys, jewelry, or small trinkets.
- **Embroidered Wall Art**: Create embroidered hoop art by stitching intricate designs or inspirational quotes onto fabric stretched in embroidery hoops. Hang them on the wall for a charming and personalized touch.
- **Hand-Painted Rocks**: Decorate smooth river rocks or pebbles with acrylic paint to create colorful designs, patterns, or miniature landscapes. Scatter them in your garden or use them as paperweights.

- **Felted Soap Bars**: Wrap bars of soap in colorful wool roving and felt them by hand to create felted soap bars. The wool acts as a gentle exfoliant and makes the soap last longer.
- **Scented Sachets**: Sew fabric sachets filled with aromatic herbs, dried flowers, or potpourri. Place them in drawers, closets, or under pillows to add a pleasant fragrance to your home.
- **Paper Quilling Art**: Create intricate designs and patterns using paper quilling techniques. Roll and shape strips of colored paper to make decorative motifs, flowers, or abstract designs.
- **Embroidered Fabric Bookmarks**: Stitch colorful designs or patterns onto fabric scraps to make personalized bookmarks. Add ribbons or tassels for an extra touch.
- **Beaded Wind Chimes**: String colorful beads onto wire or fishing line to make beaded wind chimes. Hang them outdoors to add visual interest and soothing sounds to your garden or patio.
- **Pressed Leaf Suncatchers**: Press colorful leaves between sheets of wax paper or laminating sheets, and frame them to create vibrant suncatchers. Hang them in windows to catch the sunlight.
- **Clay Pot Critters**: Paint and decorate clay pots to resemble animals, insects, or mythical creatures. Use them as whimsical garden decorations or planters for small succulents or herbs.

These unique small craft ideas offer plenty of opportunities to explore your creativity, learn new skills, and create beautiful handmade items to cherish or share with others. Whether you enjoy working with fabric, paper, wood, or other materials, there's something for every craft enthusiast to enjoy in retirement.

Tie Dyeing

Tie-dyeing is a colorful and creative craft that involves adding vibrant designs and patterns to fabric using dyes and a variety of tying and folding techniques.

Our dispersed family used to get together for "Thanksmas." That was our name for Christmas at Thanksgiving. We did this because no one wanted to risk driving hundreds of miles in potentially treacherous December snowstorms. Besides, most everyone wanted to be home for Christmas.

We often had a gift exchange where we submitted ideas to a designated coordinator, who semi-randomly selected who traded presents with whom and passed along the suggestion list to that person. I had a tie-dye shirt on my list. My niece was paired with me. Since the list was merely a suggestion, she got me a small tie-dye kit and a few cotton T-shirts. Ugh! So, that meant I had to do it myself.

The last time I had attempted to do any tie-dyeing was when I was a teen in the wild 70s using Rit dye. The results were okay at the time, but not very fancy, and the colors were muted. And, of course, I was just winging it. I had no idea what I was doing.

This new kit had vibrant colors and actual instructions. I then went to YouTube and looked for additional techniques, patterns, and tips. I created my three shirts and was pleased with the variety of colors and patterns I had created.

I liked the process enough that I ordered more dye and other supplies. Over the years, I have probably made 50 T-shirts and some sweatshirts. During the pandemic, I tie-dyed about 40 cotton face masks, many of which I sold on Etsy.

 Here's an explanation of how tie-dyeing works:

- **Materials**: To start tie-dyeing, you'll need a few basic materials:

  - *Fabric*: Choose 100% cotton. I only dye pure cotton. The dyes I use will not adhere to synthetics. However, the stitching in store-bought 100% cotton T-shirts is actually a cotton blend or synthetic, and it will not take the dye. I am okay with that, and that is what I use. But if you are really picky, you can order T-shirts online that are 100% cotton, including the stitching.

- *Dyes*: Use fabric dyes specifically made for tie-dyeing. These dyes come in a variety of colors and can be purchased as liquids or powders. (I always get powders and mix them myself. The mixture only has a shelf life of about three weeks. So, just mix what you will use immediately.)
- *Soda Ash*: This is a chemical fixative that helps the dye bond to the fabric. It's usually mixed with water to create a solution for soaking the fabric before dyeing.
- *Tools*: Gather items like rubber bands, string, or plastic squeeze bottles for applying the dye. You may also need gloves, aprons, and plastic sheeting to protect your workspace.

- **Preparation**: Before dyeing, prepare your fabric by washing and drying it to remove any dirt, sizing, or finishes that might interfere with the dyeing process. If you're using a premade tie-dye kit, follow the instructions provided for preparing the fabric. [After the T-shirt comes out of the washer, I soak it in a combination of soda ash and urea (fertilizer) for half an hour. The soda ash opens up the fibers, and the urea is a wetting agent that allows the fibers to take the dye much more intensely.]

- **Tying and Folding**: The key to tie-dyeing is creating interesting patterns by folding, twisting, and tying the fabric in different ways. There are many techniques to experiment with, including:

  - **Spiral**: Twist the fabric into a spiral shape, and secure it with rubber bands. (Most of the time, I just do the spiral.)
  - **Crumple**: Crumple the fabric into a ball, and secure it with rubber bands.
  - **Accordion**: Fold the fabric into accordion-like pleats, and secure them with rubber bands.
  - **Shibori**: Use traditional Japanese tie-dyeing techniques to create intricate patterns with stitching, folding, and binding.

- **Dyeing**: Once your fabric is tied and folded, it's time to apply the dye. Mix the fabric dyes according to the manufacturer's instructions, and transfer them to squeeze bottles for easy application. [I also add urea (fertilizer) to the dye to further enhance the dye getting into the fibers.] Apply the dye to the fabric, saturating it thoroughly and adding multiple colors, if desired.
- **Setting the Dye:** After dyeing, it's important to set the colors to ensure they won't fade or wash out. This typically involves wrapping the dyed fabric in plastic wrap or a plastic bag to keep it moist, then allowing it to sit for several hours or overnight. This allows the dye to penetrate and bond with the fabric fibers. (I have a gas oven from the 60s that has a pilot light, so it is always a little warm. I put the item in a plastic grocery bag and let it sit in the oven for about 24 hours—but no more.)
- **Rinsing and Washing**: Once the dye has set, you can remove the rubber bands, unfold the fabric, and rinse the fabric under cold water to remove excess dye. Gradually increase the water temperature until it runs clear. (This is when the article transforms from an ugly-looking mess and starts to exhibit the truly glorious colors. Rinsing takes a long time before it starts to run clear, so be patient.) Then, wash the fabric in warm water with a mild detergent to remove any remaining dye and soda ash. Finally, dry the fabric according to the manufacturer's instructions. (Once it's dry, you can finally appreciate the masterpiece you created. This is the point where it finally has its finished appearance.)

Overall, tie-dyeing is a fun and versatile craft that allows for endless creativity and experimentation. Whether you're creating bold, psychedelic designs or delicate, intricate patterns, tie-dyeing offers a colorful way to express yourself and add a personal touch to clothing, accessories, and home décor items.

Chapter 4
Learn Something New

"Do not grow old, no matter how long you live. Never cease to stand like curious children before the great mystery into which we were born."

—Albert Einstein

Now that you have the time, perhaps you would like to pick up a new skill. Few things are as satisfying as becoming proficient at something that you were unable to do previously. Think how free you felt when you learned how to ride a bike as a kid. Or how proud you were when you learned how to whistle. Or how much joy it brought you when you learned how to belch at will. Oh, you didn't master that? Well, that is something you really must master before you can be a complete person. My point is that there are many skills that can be quite fun once you get the hang of it.

Usually when you start, you are frustrated because you are no good at it and the skill seems unattainable. So many people quit at this exact moment and have no clue that they just threw away a gift. Yes, a gift. This may sound weird, but I had an epiphany about this stage. This is a unique point in time. You need to take a moment and savor this uncomfortable, frustrating stage.

It is very exciting to take that first uncomfortable step. You pick up a guitar or sit down at a piano and can't play anything that sounds like a song. You pick up a real camera with lots of settings you've never heard of, and you don't even know how to turn it on. Or you get a 3D printer, and everything about it is frustrating and foreign.

This is when I find that very special delight that I will never, ever have again with that activity. This is the moment where I know nothing, and I have to learn what it is about. One step at a time, I start to understand how to make it work to get the results I want. I absolutely love this stage because this is where I am challenged.

This should never hold you back. I think a lot of people meet these obstacles and abandon the activity because they think it is hard. It may be difficult, and it may take practice, but this is where you can enjoy some of the greatest personal reward. You probably don't want to fight with something for many hours at a time. Just take a break and work on it a little the next day. Many things that are new to you are not going to be easy the first time you try.

Embrace the challenge. There are so many resources available these days, such as books, YouTube, Google, clubs, blogs, and others. You may find you absolutely love something once you get the hang of it. But you will also feel a personal accomplishment for having started at the point of knowing zero and progressing to proficiency.

Let me put it another way, drawing from my experience as a serial hobbyist. I love this stage because it is unique. It almost makes me tingle because my head is so vacant. I know nothing! How sweet is this moment! It is so peculiar. I will never be back this way again. I am only going to know more tomorrow than I know today about this skill. And the vacuum will have vanished. Gone! I know I will never be this mystified again about this thing. As long as I keep moving forward, I will never face these same challenges.

But once I have some proficiency in the skill, I may start to get bored with it. I sometimes lose interest in one thing when something new piques my interest. After that, maybe the skill is also incredibly fun and I continue with it or maybe it is just medium fun and I can't make time for it.

Isn't that funny? To me, that frustrating start is sometimes the most fun. That vacuum, that dumbfounded ignorance is a rush.

You don't have enough time to do everything at once. So, when the newness and fun fade, it's okay to put it down and pick up something else. This has been my own experience. I may like something for a few months or a few years, but when I feel like doing something else, I give myself permission. I may come back to it in a few months or years or I may not. Either way, I learned a lot about it while I was involved with it, and it became a part of me. To me, that is very special. I can look inside and see all of these rooms I built with abilities and experiences. I am full and rich inside with so many different talents I've picked up along the way.

Learn Guitar

Learning guitar can be an incredibly rewarding journey, whether you're a complete beginner or someone with a musical background. This is an instrument that is near and dear to my heart.

I was probably in fourth grade, and our class had show-and-tell on Fridays. One classmate brought in a black and white Sears Silvertone electric guitar with an amplifier built right into the guitar case. He played a song or two for the class, and, instantly, I knew I wanted to learn how to play.

My parents got me lessons at a local music store. My instructor used Mel Bay lesson books. Then, I started jamming with another of my friends in school, and we formed a band. That shaped my social trajectory through high school in the early 70s and a little beyond. I had so many great times with so many fun people. Now, I am one of those hopeless musicians with more guitars than time to play, and I am happy with that predicament.

My point is, a musical instrument is fun to play. You can play your favorite songs, and you can interact with other musical people, whether they play instruments or just love music. It is never too late to start.

First, you'll need a guitar to practice on. Acoustic guitars and electric guitars are the two main types. Acoustic guitars are typically recommended for beginners because they don't require an amplifier, whereas electric guitars need one to be heard properly. Choose the type that best suits your preferences and budget.

I rented a Harmony Stella acoustic guitar when I took my first lessons. It was a horrible guitar, but it forced me to work harder to finger the notes, and maybe it built character or made me a better guitarist.

Now, there is a whole cult around these guitars. A few years ago, I fished one out of somebody's trash pile at the curb. They were moving out, and it was a piece of detritus they were jettisoning from their lives. I refurbished it, and it is still a terrible guitar, but it is sentimental.

My advice is to find a guitar that is easy to play. It may be difficult to make that assessment as a newbie. So, you may want to enlist a guitarist friend to help you make a more informed decision. In general, electric guitars are easier to play than acoustics. But many acoustics do not take much additional effort. It is entirely up to you. You probably want to stick with an inexpensive guitar to start your journey. There is absolutely no reason to buy an expensive guitar when you are first learning.

Familiarize yourself with the different parts of the guitar, such as the body, neck, frets, bridge, strings, and tuners. Learn how to hold the guitar properly, with the body resting on your right leg (if you're right-handed) or your left leg (if you're left-handed). Practice holding the pick (if you're using one) and positioning your fingers on the fretboard.

Here is my advice to lefties. If you are only moderately left-handed and you perform many tasks the same as any right-handed person, then try learning on a right-handed guitar. You should be able to learn just fine, and you will have a world of guitars available to you when you want to move up. However, if you are hard-core left-handed, then you probably should buy a left-handed guitar. Don't pull a Jimi Hendrix and flip a right-handed guitar upside down. That is madness.

Before you start playing, it's essential to tune your guitar. You can use a tuner device, a tuning app on your smartphone, or tune by ear using a reference pitch. The standard tuning for a guitar is E-A-D-G-B-E (from the thickest string to the thinnest), but there are other alternate tunings as well.

Begin by learning some basic chords, such as G, C, D, E, A, and F. Practice switching between these chords smoothly and accurately. Start with simple strumming patterns and focus on getting a clear sound from each chord.

Consistent practice is key to improving your guitar skills. Set aside time each day to practice, even if it's just for a few minutes. Focus on practicing chords, scales, and songs that you enjoy playing.

Consider taking guitar lessons from a qualified instructor, either in person or online. A teacher can provide personalized guidance, feedback, and structured lessons tailored to your skill level and goals. They can also help you avoid common mistakes and develop good playing habits.

Understanding music theory will greatly enhance your ability to play guitar. Learn about scales, intervals, chord progressions, and rhythm patterns. This knowledge will help you understand how music works and make it easier to learn new songs and create your own music.

Learning to play songs is a fun and motivating way to practice guitar. Start with easy songs that have simple chord progressions and strumming patterns. As you progress, challenge yourself with more complex songs and techniques.

There are many resources available to help you learn guitar, including books, online tutorials, instructional videos, and guitar tablature (tabs). Take advantage of these resources to supplement your learning, and explore different styles and techniques.

Learning guitar takes time and dedication, so be patient with yourself and don't get discouraged if you encounter difficulties along the way. Be persistent, keep practicing regularly, and celebrate your progress as you continue to improve.

Remember that learning guitar is a journey, and everyone progresses at their own pace. Enjoy the process, stay curious, and have fun making music!

Learn Keyboard

Learning keyboard, like learning any musical instrument, requires dedication, practice, and patience.

You'll need access to a keyboard or piano to practice on. If you don't have one, consider purchasing a keyboard or electric piano. Keyboards come in various sizes and styles, ranging from full-size digital pianos with weighted keys to smaller, portable keyboards with fewer features.

Take some time to familiarize yourself with the layout of the keyboard. A standard keyboard has 88 keys, including white and black keys. The white keys represent the natural notes (A, B, C, D, E, F, G), while the black keys represent the sharps and flats (e.g., A#, C#, D#, etc.).

Understanding basic music theory will help you make sense of the keyboard and how music is structured. Learn about notes, scales, chords, and rhythm. Start with the fundamentals, and gradually build your knowledge as you progress.

Learn the proper hand and finger positioning for playing the keyboard. Sit up straight with your feet flat on the floor, and position your hands comfortably on the keyboard. Practice proper finger placement and posture to avoid tension and strain.

Begin with simple exercises to develop your finger strength, dexterity, and coordination. Practice playing scales, arpeggios, and finger exercises to improve your technique and control.

Familiarize yourself with basic chords, such as major and minor triads. Practice playing chord progressions and switching smoothly between chords. Start with simple songs that use basic chords to accompany melodies.

Sight-reading is the ability to read and play music notation in real time. Practice reading sheet music and playing simple melodies on the keyboard. Start with easy pieces, and gradually increase the difficulty as you improve.

Take advantage of learning resources, such as beginner piano books, online tutorials, instructional videos, and educational apps. These resources can provide structured lessons, exercises, and guidance to help you learn at your own pace.

Consider taking keyboard lessons from a qualified instructor, either in person or online. A teacher can provide personalized instruction, feedback, and support tailored to your learning style and goals. They can also help you develop good practice habits and address any challenges you encounter.

Consistent practice is essential for progress. Set aside time each day to practice keyboard, even if it's just for a few minutes. Focus on building your skills gradually, and enjoy the process of learning and making music.

Remember that learning keyboard is a journey, and progress takes time. Be patient, stay motivated, and have fun exploring the beautiful world of music!

Learn Harmonica

Learning to play harmonica can be a fun and rewarding journey. I started learning a little bit of harmonica a few years ago. I have not gone far with it, but I can say that spending a little more money on a harmonica seems to be necessary in order to get a model that bends the notes easier and that is just generally more responsive to play.

Years ago, a harmonica was just a toy that you could purchase very cheaply. They have evolved, and so have the prices. Also, remember the reeds in a harmonica have a life. When the reeds reach the end of their life, some artists replace the harmonica, while others replace just the reed plates.

For me, at the time of this writing, the Hohner Special 20 is a nice balance between price and performance. But ask around for the advice of performers you may encounter. Everyone has an opinion, and their insight is valuable.

Harmonicas come in different keys and types. The most common type for beginners is the diatonic harmonica, which is typically tuned to a specific key (e.g., C, G, A). Start with a harmonica in the key of C, as it's the most versatile and is commonly used for beginner instruction.

Take a moment to familiarize yourself with the harmonica's layout. A diatonic harmonica has multiple holes (usually 10); and each hole produces two different notes, one when you exhale (blow) and one when you inhale (draw). Learn to identify the blow and draw notes for each hole.

Start by learning some basic techniques for playing the harmonica:

- Single Notes: Practice isolating individual notes by puckering your lips tightly around a single hole while blocking adjacent holes with your tongue or lips.
- Bending Notes: Experiment with bending notes by altering the shape of your mouth and changing the air pressure to produce lower pitches on draw notes.
- Tongue Blocking: Explore the tongue blocking technique, where you use your tongue to block multiple holes at once to play chords and octaves.
- Hand Effects: Experiment with hand effects, such as cupping, wah-wah, and flutter tongue to vary the tone and texture of your sound.

Harmonica playing relies heavily on proper breath control. Practice breathing from your diaphragm and maintaining a steady airflow while playing. Focus on controlling the volume and intensity of your breath to produce clear and consistent tones.

Start by learning some simple scales and melodies on the harmonica. Practice playing scales up and down the instrument to improve your finger coordination and muscle memory. Then, learn some easy songs or melodies to play along with.

Take advantage of learning resources such as harmonica instruction books, online tutorials, instructional videos, and educational apps. These resources can provide structured lessons, exercises, and guidance to help you learn at your own pace.

Practice playing along with your favorite songs and tracks. Listen carefully to the melodies, and try to replicate them on your harmonica. Playing along with music is a great way to develop your ear and timing skills.

Record yourself playing, and listen back to identify areas for improvement. Pay attention to your tone, timing, and technique, and strive to refine your playing over time.

Connect with other harmonica players through online forums, social media groups, or local harmonica clubs. Sharing tips, experiences, and music with others can be inspiring and motivating.

Learning the harmonica takes time and practice, so be patient with yourself and enjoy the process. Celebrate your progress along the way, and embrace the joy of making music with this versatile and expressive instrument.

With dedication, practice, and a love for music, you'll soon be playing your favorite tunes and exploring the endless possibilities of the harmonica.

Learn Ukulele

Learning the ukulele can be a lot of fun+ whether you're a complete beginner or have some musical background. My mom had a ukulele, and I played around with it as a kid, but I never really learned anything. So, a few years ago, I decided that I needed to change. I went to my favorite music store, tried out the selection of ukuleles they had on the wall, and picked out the one I liked. It is not electric, and I love it.

You might wonder about the tiny neck and tiny frets and think it is going to be crowded with all of your fingers trying to dance around on there. I invite you to view a YouTube of Israel Kamakawiwoʻole (affectionately referred to as just "IZ") performing his version of "Somewhere Over the Rainbow." You will likely never hear a more beautiful rendition, and he was a very large man with large hands. I think this is evidence that most people will find there is enough room on the fingerboard for them.

First, you'll need a ukulele to practice on. Ukuleles come in various sizes and types, including soprano, concert, tenor, and baritone. Choose the size and type that best suits your preferences and budget. For beginners, a soprano or concert ukulele is recommended due to its smaller size and ease of playability.

Take some time to familiarize yourself with the parts of the ukulele, including the body, neck, frets, strings, and tuning pegs. Learn how to hold the ukulele properly, with the body resting against your chest and the neck angled upward at a comfortable angle.

Before you start playing, it's essential to tune your ukulele. The standard tuning for a ukulele is G-C-E-A (from the top string to the bottom string). You can use a tuner device, a tuning app on your smartphone, or tune by ear using a reference pitch. You may want to sing "My Dog Has Fleas" as you pluck each string. It is difficult not to.

Begin by learning some basic ukulele chords, such as C, G, F, Am, and Dm. Practice forming these chords and smoothly switching between them. Start with simple strumming patterns, and focus on getting a clear sound from each chord.

Practice different strumming patterns and picking techniques to develop your rhythmic skills and finger coordination. Experiment with various strumming directions, speeds, and dynamics to create different sounds and textures.

Start playing simple songs that use basic chords and strumming patterns. There are many beginner-friendly songs available online, including traditional folk songs, pop tunes, and nursery rhymes. Choose songs that you enjoy and that match your skill level.

Take advantage of learning resources, such as beginner ukulele books, online tutorials, instructional videos, and educational apps. These resources can provide structured lessons, exercises, and guidance to help you learn at your own pace.

Consider taking ukulele lessons from a qualified instructor, either in person or online. A teacher can provide personalized instruction, feedback, and support tailored to your learning style and goals. They can also help you develop good practice habits and address any challenges you encounter.

Consistent practice is essential for progress. Set aside time each day to practice ukulele, even if it's just for a few minutes. Focus on building your skills gradually, and enjoy the process of learning and making music.

Learning the ukulele is a journey, so be patient with yourself and enjoy the process. Celebrate your progress along the way, and embrace the joy of making music with this delightful and versatile instrument.

With dedication, practice, and a love for music, you'll soon be strumming your favorite tunes and exploring the endless possibilities of the ukulele.

Learn Knitting

Learning to knit can be a rewarding and relaxing hobby. My mom tried teaching me to knit when I was probably five. I don't believe I got the hang of it, but several years ago, I decided I wanted to revisit this skill. I had decided but did not do anything about it until my wife got me a set of knitting needles and a knitting book for Christmas. The book was really good as a reference, but I ended up watching lots of YouTube tutorials to learn the stitches. She had some acrylic yarn sitting around, so I practiced with that. These were aluminum needles, and they were just too slick for me. I kept dropping stitches and sometimes whole rows. So, I got some bamboo needles. These have a little more drag, and I find them much easier to control.

I initially started knitting in the English style, which involves holding the yarn in your right hand. It is horrible because you must take your hand off of the needle to wrap the yarn for each stitch. It is so tiresome and slow. I eventually found a channel that demonstrated how to do flicking. With this technique, you hold the yarn in your right hand, but you never let go of the needle. You may have to practice it for a while before it feels natural, but it is worth it. It is so much faster, smoother, and less tiring. I encourage everyone to try that technique.

If you're a guy, you may be uncomfortable with this hobby, but I am here to tell you there are several guys that knit. I see them in YouTube videos, so from that, I know for a certainty they exist.

My first project was to knit a wool scarf using a 4-row repeat pattern with multicolor yarn. I got the pattern out of sync at one point and had to rip out several dozen rows. But when it was finished, it was beautiful and very warm.

The greatest reward I have with this hobby is knitting baby blankets for relatives who are increasing their family units. To hold all of the stitches, I found it easier to get a 40-inch circular knitting needle. Mine has two small bamboo needles at either end of a thick nylon filament. Circular needles are often used for knitting in the round. You do this to knit socks or beanies. But you can just as easily use them to knit flat articles like baby blankets. For my first blanket, I chose a 12-row repeat pattern of purl and knit stitches that gave the blanket a zigzag relief pattern.

I grossly miscalculated the stitch count for this first baby blanket and ended up with something that could just about cover an entire twin bed. So, I suppose it was more of a youth blanket. I simplified my pattern to the garter stitch, which is simply knit stitching every row. I also drastically reduced my stitch count for my next blanket.

By using my 40-inch circular needle, I can knit lengthwise on the blanket instead of knitting on the short side. This produces ribs that run the length of the blanket, and I think that looks nice. I just select whatever seems to be the prettiest polyester baby blanket yarn I can find at the fabric store. I send the blanket when the lucky couple has their baby, and my hope is that they treasure the blanket as an heirloom and pass it down in the family.

My point is that this hobby can be satisfying in a very unique way. You and others can wear your creations. You can knit dishcloths that you and others can use. You can even create family heirlooms.

To begin knitting, you'll need some basic materials. These typically include knitting needles and yarn. For beginners, it's recommended to start with medium-sized knitting needles (US size 8 or 9) and a smooth, medium-weight yarn in a light color that's easy to see.

Familiarize yourself with the basic terminology and techniques of knitting. Learn about terms such as cast on, knit stitch, purl stitch, and bind off. There are many online tutorials, books, and videos available that can help you learn the fundamentals of knitting.

Casting on is the process of creating the foundation row of stitches on your knitting needle. There are several methods for casting on, including the long-tail cast on, knitted cast on, and cable cast on. Choose a method that feels comfortable to you, and practice casting on a few rows of stitches.

The knit stitch is the most basic stitch in knitting. Once you've cast on your stitches, practice knitting by inserting the needle into the first stitch on your left needle, wrapping the yarn around the needle, and pulling the new loop through to create a new stitch on your right needle. Repeat this process across the row.

The purl stitch is another fundamental knitting stitch. Practice purling by inserting the needle into the first stitch on your left needle from right to left, wrapping the yarn around the needle, and pulling the new loop through to create a new stitch on your right needle. Repeat this process across the row.

Once you've mastered the knit and purl stitches individually, practice combining them to create different stitch patterns. Experiment with alternating knit and purl stitches to create ribbing, a seed stitch, stockinette stitch, and other textured patterns. There are so many different stitches. It is fun to browse various YouTube channels to see examples and download patterns.

Start knitting simple projects to practice your skills and build your confidence. There are many beginner-friendly knitting patterns available online or in books, including scarves, dishcloths, hats, and baby blankets. Choose a project that matches your skill level and interests.

Consider joining a knitting group or community to connect with other knitters, share tips and techniques, and get inspiration for your projects. Knitting groups often meet in person or online to knit together, swap patterns, and socialize.

As you gain experience, try experimenting with different types of yarns, colors, textures, and needle sizes to expand your skills and create unique projects. Each yarn and needle combination will produce a different result, so don't be afraid to explore and try new things.

Like any skill, knitting takes time and practice to master. Set aside time each day or week to practice knitting, even if it's just for a few minutes. Be patient with yourself, and celebrate your progress as you continue to improve and develop your knitting skills.

Remember that knitting is a versatile and creative hobby that can be enjoyed by people of all ages and skill levels. Enjoy the process of learning and creating beautiful handmade items with your own two hands!

Learn Origami

Starting an origami hobby is a wonderful way to explore creativity and mindfulness through the art of paper folding. I was minding my own business, just wandering around the Ohio State Fair some years ago with my wife, and we went into one of the buildings where there were all sorts of exhibits. I noticed a table where they had some paper models set up, and a lady was folding paper. They had chairs scattered around, so I sat down and started chatting with the lady. She shoved some colored paper in front of me and walked me through folding a simple component that could be assembled into a modular model.

That was really fun, and I was hooked. Now, I prefer models that require just one piece of square paper. In the beginning, I would use 8.5" x 8.5" paper squares cut down from regular 8.5" x 11" copy paper. Now, I like thin, crisp origami paper that is 6" x 6". But sometimes, for a really complex model, I will use a piece of 12" x 12" origami paper. I have memorized various birds, flowers, and geometric models. I have done many one-offs, including complex tessellations. There are probably thousands of YouTube videos demonstrating how to fold different models. That is my favorite way to learn folding. Most people really love it when you hand them a finished piece. If you don't hand them out, you end up with bags and bags of models. You can only display so many.

One of my favorite things to do is take a few pieces of origami paper with me when I have an appointment and I will be sitting in a waiting room. I also like to take paper when I have a flight. I have perfected my ability to fold paper in midair. I do not need a flat surface. This removes my biggest aggravation when trying to fold outside the home. Since I don't need a table, my hobby is completely portable. I pre-fold a few pieces of paper so they fit in my pocket, and I am ready to go.

Of course, if you just want to look at your phone while you're waiting or on a flight, that is fine. But I find this to be a great alternative.

Begin by familiarizing yourself with basic origami terminology, techniques, and symbols. Learn about terms like valley fold, mountain fold, crease, and reverse fold. Understand the symbols used in origami diagrams to represent different folding actions.

You'll need some basic supplies to start folding origami. All you need is square paper, but you can also use specialty origami paper, which is thinner and easier to fold. You can purchase origami paper in various colors, patterns, and sizes from craft stores or online. Alternatively, you can cut square sheets of paper from larger sheets using scissors or a paper cutter.

Begin with simple origami models that are suitable for beginners. Some easy models to start with include the traditional crane, frog, boat, and flower. These models typically involve basic folds and are great for practicing fundamental origami techniques.

Use origami diagrams, tutorials, books, or online resources to learn how to fold different origami models. Follow step-by-step instructions carefully, paying attention to the orientation of the paper and the sequence of folds. Take your time and practice each fold until you feel comfortable with it before moving on to the next step.

Practice folding origami regularly to improve your skills and gain confidence. Experiment with different types of paper, sizes, and designs. Don't be discouraged if your early folds don't turn out perfectly. Like any skill, origami takes practice and patience to master.

Join online origami communities, forums, or social media groups to connect with other origami enthusiasts, share tips and advice, and showcase your creations. Participating in the origami community can provide inspiration, support, and motivation as you continue your origami journey.

Once you've mastered basic folds and models, start experimenting with more complex designs and techniques. Explore advanced origami models, modular origami, tessellations, and origami design. Challenge yourself to create your own original origami designs and patterns.

Share your origami creations with friends, family, and the origami community. Display your finished models in your home or give them as gifts to loved ones. Consider photographing or documenting your origami creations to keep a record of your progress and inspire others.

Consider attending origami workshops, classes, or conventions to learn from experienced origami artists and instructors. Participating in hands-on workshops can provide valuable insights, techniques, and inspiration to enhance your origami skills.

Above all, enjoy the process of folding origami and the meditative quality it brings. Embrace the beauty of each fold and the satisfaction of creating something beautiful from a simple sheet of paper. Origami is not only a creative hobby but also a mindful practice that can bring joy, relaxation, and focus to your life.

Starting an origami hobby is a delightful journey of exploration and creativity that offers endless possibilities for artistic expression and personal growth. With dedication, practice, and an open mind, you'll discover the joy and beauty of origami folding.

Learn 3D Printing

Starting a 3D printing hobby can be an exciting and rewarding journey into the world of digital fabrication. Just a few years ago, I got into this hobby because a separate project I was working on took a funny turn that necessitated creating custom plastic parts.

Oh, okay, you forced it out of me. The backstory is that I wanted to learn how to program microcontroller boards, like the Arduino. So somehow, my wife knew the exact learning kit to get me as a Christmas present. There may have been an online list somewhere that I neglected to hide. Anyway, once I had the kit, I needed a suitable project to use all of the sensors and end up with something I would enjoy. That was when I found a *Squid Game* doll project online.

The *Squid Game* doll's name is Young-hee. The *Squid Game* is a TV show that may be a bit violent for some people, but in this particular project, Young-hee simply plays Red Light, Green Light, and no one actually dies when they lose. This seemed like the perfect project because the end result is very creepy.

I got a nice amateur/hobbyist level 3D printer that was large enough to print the legs and other tall parts of the doll. I knew there was going to be a learning curve because I had seen many tales of woe online, and I knew the company and model I selected was going to come with some of that initial setup drama. But I also knew this printer was amazing once it was dialed in.

Let me break this down. Some brands and models are almost plug-n-play. But typically, you are going to pay more for those printers. I was already over budget with the model I selected, and I knew there were oodles of resources online to help me get past the little bumps.

I was working at the time, so I had limited time to spend on the project. It ended up taking several weeks to dial in the settings and learn the software, but I ended up printing the entire doll successfully, painting it, programming the board, installing the sensors, and it is awesome. The entire project with programming and debugging took over 200 hours, and I am over the moon happy with the creation. I could not have done it without a 3D printer. I have since used it for all kinds of things. 3D printers open an entire world of creativity.

Begin by researching 3D printing technology and understanding how it works. Learn about the different types of 3D printers, materials, software, and applications. There are plenty of online resources, tutorials, forums, and books available to help you learn the basics of 3D printing.

Decide on the type of 3D printer that best suits your needs and budget. There are several types of 3D printers available, including Fused Deposition Modeling (FDM), Stereolithography (SLA), and Digital Light Processing (DLP) printers. Consider factors such as print quality, build volume, ease of use, and cost when choosing a 3D printer. For my project, I got a model that extrudes a single filament. I used PLA plastic. But technology is advancing very quickly, and you will benefit by surveying the current field of models available at your desired price point.

Find a suitable workspace for your 3D printer, preferably in a well-ventilated area with access to power and a stable surface. Set up your 3D printer according to the manufacturer's instructions, and ensure that it is properly calibrated and leveled before starting your first print. I found I got better results by shielding my printer from drafts, so I constructed an enclosure. Some printers come with an enclosure.

Familiarize yourself with 3D modeling software, which is used to create or modify digital 3D models. There are many free and paid 3D modeling software options available, such as Tinkercad, Fusion 360, Blender, and SketchUp. Start by learning the basics of 3D modeling, and practice creating simple objects and designs.

Once you're comfortable with 3D modeling, you can start downloading or creating 3D models to print. There are many online repositories and marketplaces where you can find a wide variety of free and paid 3D models, such as Thingiverse, MyMiniFactory, and Cults. You can also create your own designs or modify existing ones to suit your needs.

Before printing, you'll need to prepare your 3D models using slicing software. Slicing software converts your 3D models into a series of thin layers and generates the instructions (G-code) needed to print them. Common slicing software options include Cura, Slic3r, and PrusaSlicer. Configure the slicing settings according to your printer and material specifications.

Once your 3D model is sliced and prepared, you can start printing it on your 3D printer. Load the filament or resin into your printer, initiate the print job using the printer's interface or software, and monitor the progress of the print. Be patient, as 3D printing can take some time, depending on the complexity and size of the object. In my experience, you may get a failed print, and that is perfectly normal, especially when you are first learning how to control the printer. As you gain experience, failures become much less frequent.

After your 3D print is complete, you may need to perform some post-processing steps to clean up and finish the object. This may include removing support structures, sanding, painting, or applying other finishing techniques to achieve the desired appearance and quality.

As you gain experience with 3D printing, don't be afraid to experiment with different materials, settings, and techniques to improve your prints. Keep learning and exploring new possibilities in the world of 3D printing.

Join online forums, social media groups, and local maker spaces to connect with other 3D printing enthusiasts, share tips and advice, and showcase your creations. The 3D printing community is supportive and collaborative, and you'll find plenty of inspiration and support as you continue your 3D printing journey.

Starting a 3D printing hobby is an exciting adventure that allows you to unleash your creativity and bring your ideas to life in three dimensions. With some patience, practice, and experimentation, you'll be well on your way to mastering the art of 3D printing and creating amazing objects of your own.

Learn How to Program a Microcontroller Board

If you are a little bit techie, you might find this quite fun. Arduino is one of the most popular microcontroller boards out there. So, I will focus on that as a starting point for this hobby. Learning to program an Arduino can be a rewarding experience and open up opportunities to create a wide range of electronic projects. As I mentioned in the above section about 3D printing, I received a complete Arduino learning kit as a Christmas present and then found a project online to incorporate it into a *Squid Game* doll that I 3D printed and painted. It plays Red Light, Green Light. It talks, its head rotates, it has sensors that determine the distance and movement of players, its eyes change color, it responds to a handheld remote, and has a countdown timer on the front. The end result is magnificently creepy, and I was totally delighted.

The first step is to obtain an Arduino board. There are several models available, but the most common one for beginners is the Arduino Uno. You can purchase an Arduino board online or from an electronics store.

Download and install the Arduino Integrated Development Environment (IDE) on your computer. The Arduino IDE is available for

Windows, macOS, and Linux and can be downloaded for free from the Arduino website. Once installed, launch the IDE.

Connect your Arduino board to your computer using a USB cable. The IDE should automatically detect the board and select the appropriate port. If not, you may need to manually select the board and port from the "Tools" menu.

Familiarize yourself with the basics of Arduino programming by exploring the official Arduino website, tutorials, and documentation. Learn about the Arduino programming language, which is based on C/C++, and understand concepts, such as variables, data types, functions, and control structures (e.g., loops, conditional statements).

Begin by working on simple Arduino projects to practice your programming skills. Start with projects that involve blinking an LED, reading a sensor, or controlling a servo motor. There are many beginner-friendly Arduino projects and tutorials available online to help you get started.

The Arduino IDE comes with a collection of example sketches (programs) that demonstrate various Arduino capabilities and functions. Explore these example sketches to learn how to use different Arduino libraries and components.

Once you're comfortable with the basics, start experimenting with sensors, modules, and other electronic components. Learn how to interface different sensors (e.g., temperature sensors, motion sensors) and modules (e.g., LCD displays, Wi-Fi modules) with the Arduino board.

Arduino libraries are pre-written code that simplifies the process of interfacing with external hardware and peripherals. Explore the wide range of Arduino libraries available online to find ones that suit your project needs. Learn how to install and use libraries in your Arduino sketches (programs).

Keep a record of your Arduino projects, including schematics, code, and notes. Documenting your projects will help you track your progress, troubleshoot issues, and replicate successful experiments in the future.

Join online forums, social media groups, and local maker communities to connect with other Arduino enthusiasts, share ideas, and seek advice. The Arduino community is supportive and collaborative, and you'll find plenty of inspiration and guidance as you continue your Arduino journey.

Learning to program an Arduino is a hands-on process that requires practice, experimentation, and perseverance. Start small, take your time to understand the fundamentals, and have fun exploring the world of Arduino programming and electronics.

Learn Laser Engraving

Starting a laser engraving hobby can be an exciting and creative endeavor. I got a small laser engraver kit several years ago. I assembled it and was able to perform a test print the same day. So, getting it to actually work is not too hard.

The movements of the laser are similar to 3D printing, and the software that runs the laser performs a similar task of defining how fine the lines will be, how fast the laser will travel, and what power will be delivered.

My laser is very low power. So, it can char things, but it is not useful for cutting out wooden parts. However, I was able to import photos that I had converted to black and white and then etch the photo onto heavy cardboard. I was also able to create a graphic that I etched onto a piece of 1x6 pine planking that I had cut. It is a lot of fun.

Begin by researching different types of laser engraving machines available on the market. There are various options, including desktop laser engravers and larger industrial-grade machines. Consider factors such as size, power, resolution, compatibility with different materials, and budget when choosing a laser engraving machine.

Laser engraving can be performed on a wide range of materials, including wood, acrylic, glass, leather, metal, and plastic. Choose materials that are suitable for laser engraving and compatible with your laser engraving machine. Experiment with different materials to see which ones produce the best results for your projects.

Next, choose design software for creating and preparing your laser engraving designs. Popular software options include Adobe Illustrator, CorelDRAW, AutoCAD, Inkscape, and SketchUp. These programs allow you to create vector graphics, text, and geometric shapes that can be engraved with precision. For my purposes, I used simpler Windows utilities to just generate an image that I would import. I did not have a need to get fancy.

Familiarize yourself with basic design principles and techniques to create laser engraving designs. Learn about concepts such as vector graphics, paths, strokes, fills, and layers. Practice creating simple designs and experimenting with different shapes, text, and effects.

Laser engraving machines emit high-intensity laser beams that can be hazardous if not used properly. Acquire appropriate safety equipment, such as safety glasses, gloves, and a ventilation system, to protect yourself from potential hazards. Follow all safety guidelines provided by the manufacturer of your laser engraving machine.

Set up your laser engraving machine according to the manufacturer's instructions. Install the software drivers and connect the machine to your computer. Calibrate the machine to ensure that it is properly aligned and focused for accurate engraving. This step is usually pretty simple.

Before starting on your main projects, practice laser engraving with test pieces of material. Experiment with different laser settings, such as power, speed, and resolution to achieve the desired engraving results. Use test engravings to fine-tune your techniques and familiarize yourself with the capabilities of your laser engraving machine. Remember, you cannot erase a mistake.

You probably want to vent your machine to the outdoors. You don't want your house to smell like a campfire. Some printers come with a cover and a special filter. Mine did not. So, I placed a fan close to it that sucked the air into a hose that led to a window. I masked off the rest of the window with cardboard.

Once you feel comfortable with the laser engraving process, start creating your first projects. Choose simple designs and materials to begin with, and gradually increase the complexity of your projects as you gain experience. Consider engraving personalized gifts, decorative items, signage, or custom products for friends, family, or customers.

Keep a record of your laser engraving projects, including photos, notes, and settings used. Documenting your work will help you track your progress, learn from your experiences, and showcase your portfolio to others.

Connect with other laser engraving enthusiasts by joining online forums, social media groups, and local maker communities. Share your projects, ask questions, and learn from others in the laser engraving community. Collaboration and networking can provide valuable insights, inspiration, and support as you continue your laser engraving hobby.

Starting a laser engraving hobby requires patience, practice, and a willingness to learn. Experiment with different materials, designs, and techniques to unlock the full creative potential of laser engraving. With time and dedication, you'll develop the skills and expertise to create beautiful and unique laser-engraved creations.

Research UFOs

Researching UFOs (Unidentified Flying Objects a.k.a. UAPs Unidentified Aerial Phenomena a.k.a. Unidentified Anomalous Phenomena) can be an intriguing pursuit, but it requires a critical and open-minded approach. What a fascinating topic. Some UFOs may be alien craft, but some may be human-built and used for human trafficking and to manipulate world events. How much is CIA disinformation? Or are these all just wild theories? The layers of the onion are many, and it can be a fascinating topic to explore. At this point, it seems impossible to ignore, but the truth is still buried very deep.

Begin by familiarizing yourself with the concept of UFOs. UFOs refer to aerial phenomena that cannot be readily identified or explained by conventional means. They may include sightings of strange lights, objects, or craft in the sky, often associated with potential extraterrestrial or otherworldly origins.

Research the history of UFO sightings, encounters, and investigations. Learn about notable cases, such as the Roswell incident, the Phoenix Lights, and the Rendlesham Forest incident. Explore historical documents, eyewitness testimonies, and government reports related to UFO sightings.

Look for scientific studies and research papers that investigate UFO phenomena from a scientific perspective. While UFOs remain a controversial topic within the scientific community, there are researchers who have conducted rigorous investigations into UFO sightings, atmospheric anomalies, and potential explanations.

Investigate declassified government documents and official investigations related to UFOs. Many governments have released previously classified documents related to UFO sightings and investigations, including the United States (through projects like Project Blue Book), Canada, the United Kingdom, and France.

Connect with reputable UFO research organizations and investigative groups that study UFO phenomena. These organizations often conduct field investigations, analyze sighting reports, and collaborate with experts in various scientific disciplines. Examples include the Mutual UFO Network (MUFON), the Center for UFO Studies (CUFOS), and the National UFO Reporting Center (NUFORC).

Attend UFO conferences, symposiums, and events to learn from experts, researchers, and eyewitnesses in the field of ufology. These gatherings provide opportunities to hear presentations, participate in panel discussions, and network with others interested in UFO research.

Consider conducting your own field investigations of UFO sightings and phenomena in your area. Interview eyewitnesses, collect data, and document any evidence or observations related to UFO sightings. Exercise caution and skepticism when evaluating eyewitness accounts and physical evidence.

Stay updated on the latest news, developments, and discoveries related to UFOs and ufology. Follow reputable sources of information, including scientific journals, news outlets, and credible websites dedicated to UFO research. Exercise critical thinking and discernment when evaluating information and claims related to UFOs.

Collaborate with experts in relevant fields, such as astronomy, physics, psychology, and aviation to gain insights into UFO phenomena from diverse perspectives. Engage in interdisciplinary discussions and research collaborations to explore potential explanations for UFO sightings and encounters.

Approach UFO research with an open mind, but also maintain a healthy dose of skepticism and critical thinking. While some UFO sightings may defy conventional explanations, not all reports are necessarily evidence of extraterrestrial visitation. Consider multiple hypotheses and explanations for UFO phenomena, and be willing to reassess your conclusions based on new evidence and information.

Researching UFOs requires patience, curiosity, and a willingness to explore the unknown. By approaching the subject with an open mind and a critical eye, you can contribute to the ongoing investigation and understanding of UFO phenomena.

Learn a New Language

Learning a new language can be an enriching and rewarding experience. And if you have dreams of traveling the world, learning even some of the language of your destination can make interactions with the locals more fun and enriching. I had some Spanish in high school and college, but I did not retain much. I had to go to Paris, France once on business, and the only French word I knew was fromage (cheese). That was not helpful. I was alone, and there were plenty of locals that did not speak English. Had I known even 100 key words in French, I would have been much better equipped for my journey and more comfortable around the people.

Of course, the people in the satellite office I was training all spoke fairly good English. It was very interesting to me as an American to see that when they ordered lunch for the office, it came with a complimentary bottle or two of wine that was all consumed before commencing work in the afternoon. Being in the culture and interacting with local people is captivating. Language makes that interaction richer.

Begin by setting clear and achievable goals for your language learning journey. Determine why you want to learn the language, whether it's for travel, work, cultural interest, or personal growth. Establish specific goals, such as achieving proficiency in speaking, reading, writing, or understanding the language.

Select the language you want to learn based on your interests, goals, and practical considerations. Consider factors such as the language's relevance to your personal or professional life, its cultural significance, and the availability of resources for learning.

Gather a variety of learning resources to support your language learning efforts. These may include textbooks, online courses, language learning apps, podcasts, audio recordings, language exchange partners, and language learning websites. Explore different resources to find ones that suit your learning style and preferences.

Begin by learning basic vocabulary and grammar structures in the language. Focus on essential words and phrases for everyday communication, such as greetings, introductions, numbers, colors, and common expressions. Learn basic grammar concepts, such as verb conjugations, sentence structure, and word order.

Practice the language regularly to reinforce your learning and build fluency. Set aside dedicated time each day or week for language practice, and immerse yourself in the language as much as possible. Practice speaking, listening, reading, and writing in the language to develop all four language skills.

Immerse yourself in the language by surrounding yourself with authentic language materials and experiences. Listen to music, watch movies or TV shows, read books or articles, and engage with native speakers in the language. Immerse yourself in the language's culture to deepen your understanding and appreciation of it.

Take advantage of language learning apps and online platforms to supplement your learning. Apps like Duolingo, Babbel, Rosetta Stone, and Memrise offer interactive lessons, exercises, quizzes, and games to help you learn and practice the language on the go.

Practice speaking the language with native speakers whenever possible. Seek out language exchange partners, conversation groups, or online language forums where you can interact with native speakers and practice your speaking skills in a supportive environment.

Set milestones and benchmarks to track your language learning progress over time. Celebrate your achievements as you reach each milestone, whether it's mastering a new vocabulary list, completing a level in your language course, or holding a conversation in the language with a native speaker.

Stay motivated and persistent in your language learning journey, even when faced with challenges or setbacks. Stay focused on your goals, and remind yourself of the reasons why you wanted to learn the language in the first place. Celebrate your progress, stay positive, and keep moving forward on your language learning path.

Learning a new language takes time, effort, and dedication, but with consistent practice and a positive attitude, you can achieve your language learning goals and open up new opportunities for personal and professional growth.

Learn Unresponsive Yo-Yo Tricks

The yo-yo hobby involves the skillful manipulation and performance of tricks with a yo-yo, a classic toy consisting of an axle connected to two disks with a string looped around the axle. The unresponsive yo-yo hobby involves the use and mastery of yo-yos that are designed to "sleep," or spin freely at the end of the string without automatically returning to the hand when tugged. Unlike traditional responsive yo-yos, which return with a simple tug, unresponsive yo-yos require specific techniques to return to the hand. Unresponsive yo-yos typically have a ball bearing ring. These yo-yos are much different from the little wooden yo-yos you may have had as a kid. These modern yo-

yos are sometime made of aluminum alloy or heavy plastic and often have an hourglass shape. They are challenging but can be incredibly fun. And when you get good at some of the tricks, you can impress your friends. Well, maybe they won't be impressed, but you'll impress yourself.

Unresponsive yo-yos allow for more advanced and technical tricks compared to responsive yo-yos. Enthusiasts can perform complex string tricks, slack tricks, and intricate combinations that require precise control and timing to execute.

Unresponsive yo-yos typically feature ball bearings or other mechanisms that reduce friction and increase spin times, allowing for longer and more dynamic tricks. This extended spin time enables performers to execute multiple tricks and sequences without the yo-yo losing momentum.

To return an unresponsive yo-yo to the hand, players must perform a technique called a "bind," which involves wrapping the string around the axle in a specific manner to create friction and induce the yo-yo to return. Mastering different bind variations is essential for controlling the yo-yo and transitioning between tricks smoothly.

Unresponsive yo-yos are often used in freestyle competitions and performances where players choreograph sequences of tricks set to music. Freestyle play allows performers to showcase their creativity, style, and technical skill through fluid and expressive yo-yo play.

Unresponsive yo-yos come in a wide variety with different shapes, sizes, weights, and materials to suit individual preferences and playing styles. Players can experiment with different yo-yo designs and configurations to find the perfect setup for their needs.

Mastering unresponsive yo-yo tricks requires dedication, practice, and perseverance. Players must develop precision, timing, and muscle memory to execute tricks with consistency and accuracy, leading to personal growth and improvement over time. My suggestion is to search the various YouTube channels where top Yo-Yo enthusiasts demonstrate exactly how to duplicate their tricks. There are so many different tricks, you will never run out of fresh material.

The unresponsive yo-yo hobby fosters a vibrant community of enthusiasts who gather at yo-yo clubs, events, and competitions to share tips, techniques, and camaraderie. Competitive players compete in freestyle and technical divisions, showcasing their skills and vying for recognition and awards.

The unresponsive yo-yo hobby is driven by innovation and creativity, with players constantly pushing the boundaries of what's possible with the toy. New tricks, concepts, and styles emerge as players experiment with different movements, mounts, and combinations, keeping the hobby fresh and exciting.

Overall, the unresponsive yo-yo hobby offers a challenging yet rewarding experience for enthusiasts seeking to push their skills to new heights. Whether you're a casual player looking to learn new tricks or a competitive player aiming for the top, the world of unresponsive yo-yoing offers endless opportunities for growth, creativity, and enjoyment.

Chapter 5
Earn a Certification

"The more that you read, the more things you will know. The more that you learn, the more places you'll go."

— Dr. Seuss

Earn a Ham Radio License

Starting a ham radio hobby can be an exciting and rewarding experience.

I never wanted a ham radio license, but as a young boy in the mid-60s, I was interested in electronics, and I wanted to build a radio-controlled toy car. I built a homebrew tube transmitter and receiver that ran on big batteries using instructions and plans from a book I purchased. The receiver would actuate a relay to control the vehicle functions. This was to be the guts of my creation. I actually got both of these built, but I needed to tune the coil in the transmitter.

In those days, you needed a piece of equipment called a grid dip meter to perform that step. I sure didn't have one, and I didn't know anyone who did. So, I asked the guy at my favorite electronics store in town if he knew anyone. He actually knew a guy who was a ham operator and thought he might have one. I reached out to the fellow. He was a phone company employee and was the nicest guy. He came over to my house and helped me tune that coil. It was glorious. I could then control the relay on my receiver.

But wait, wouldn't I like to know about ham radio? I was a little reluctant; but the fellow who helped me said there was a very active ham radio club in my town, and he invited me to one of the meetings they held in their ham shack where they had all of their big transmitters. It was on a large piece of property. They had antennas to the sky and all sorts of old radio equipment discarded out in the field.

It was pretty interesting to me, so he became my "Elmer," though I don't think the term existed at that time. He was my mentor and helped me get my novice ham license in 1969. There was a short written test, and you had to be proficient in morse code at a very slow speed. The license granted you very limited privileges, but it did get you on the air.

I got a transmitter and receiver and made a few contacts. I even went to the Dayton and Cincinnati, Ohio, hamfests a few times with a friend who was about my age. However, the license was only good for two years, and it could not be renewed. It was expected you would qualify for a better, renewable license by the time it expired, and that would grant you more privileges. I was entering high school at that point and getting interested in girls and became involved in a band. So, the license expired without me trying to get a better license. I always felt a little bad about that.

Fast forward about 50 years to when Covid was in full swing, and I decided it was time to make amends for my failing. I studied using a set of books by Craig E. "Buck," K4IA, and took numerous practice tests as well as printed out the complete set of test questions and their multiple-choice answers. They no longer test telegraphy, though it is still actively used on the air. My first test session was held outdoors so they could separate students due to Covid. I took the tests for both Technician and General Class licenses and passed those. I studied some more to prepare for my Extra Class license and passed that in July of 2020. I promptly traded in my given call sign for a vanity four-character call sign.

I then got a modest 100-watt transceiver and a nice antenna analyzer. I was able to make my own inverted V antenna out of simple antenna wire. I tuned it myself with my antenna analyzer. I was only able to put the antenna up 20 feet on the end of a pipe. It is a very limited antenna. However, from Ohio, I have been able to make contacts as far away as Antarctica and Saudi Arabia and many countries all over the world. I was even able to contact K4IA. Yes, that is Craig E. "Buck," the author of the books that helped me pass my exam. I traded QSL cards with him confirming our contact and told him how grateful I was for the terrific materials he published. I have also been able to download pictures sent by the International Space Station. How amazing and fun is that?

So, you don't need a lot of equipment to go a long distance with ham radio. But to start this journey, you need a license.

Before you begin, research the licensing requirements for amateur radio operators in your country. In the United States, for example, you'll need to obtain an Amateur Radio Technician license from the Federal Communications Commission (FCC). Look for study materials and resources to help you prepare for the licensing exam.

Once you understand the licensing requirements, begin studying for the licensing exam. There are many online resources, study guides, and practice exams available to help you prepare. Study topics such as regulations, operating procedures, radio theory, and safety practices.

Schedule a time to take the licensing exam at a local testing center. Be sure to bring any required identification and paperwork with you on the day of the exam. The exam typically consists of multiple-choice questions on topics related to amateur radio. If you pass the exam, you'll receive your amateur radio license and call sign.

After obtaining your license, choose a ham radio transceiver that meets your needs and budget. There are many types of radios available, ranging from handheld portable units to base station setups with more power and features. Consider factors such as frequency coverage, power output, modes of operation (e.g., voice, Morse code, digital), and available accessories.

Once you have your radio, set up your ham radio station at home or in a suitable location. Install antennas, connect your radio to a power source, and set up any necessary accessories, such as a microphone, headphones, or keyer. Follow safety guidelines and regulations when installing antennas and operating your radio.

Familiarize yourself with operating procedures and etiquette for amateur radio operators. Learn how to make contacts, listen for calls, identify yourself using your call sign, and follow established communication protocols. Practice proper radio etiquette, such as waiting your turn to speak and avoiding interference with other users.

Consider joining a local ham radio club or organization to connect with other amateur radio operators in your area. Clubs often offer meetings, events, activities, and resources for members, including licensing classes, equipment loans, and operating opportunities. Networking with other hams can help you learn and grow as a radio operator.

Get on the air and start making contacts with other ham radio operators. Participate in on-air activities, such as contests, special events, and public service events. Listen to different bands and modes to explore the variety of communication opportunities available in amateur radio.

Amateur radio is a lifelong learning journey. Stay engaged with the hobby by continuing to learn, exploring new technologies and operating modes, and participating in activities and events. Attend hamfests, workshops, and training sessions to expand your knowledge and skills.

Above all, enjoy the hobby of amateur radio and the camaraderie of the ham radio community. Experiment with different antennas, radios, modes, and activities to find what you enjoy most about amateur radio. Whether it's making long-distance contacts, providing emergency communications, experimenting with new technologies, or simply chatting with other hams, there's something for everyone in the world of ham radio.

Starting a ham radio hobby can be a fulfilling and enriching experience and provide opportunities for learning, friendship, and personal growth. With dedication, enthusiasm, and a willingness to learn, you can become an active and valued member of the amateur radio community.

Earn a Pilot License

Have you ever wanted to fly? Have you ever wanted to travel directly to out-of-the-way locations? As a pilot, you can fly a small plane into smaller airports that might be closer to your destination. You can make your own flight schedule.

When my wife was younger, she had a friend who was a pilot. They would sometimes take day trips to destinations like the Bahamas. On their trip to the Bahamas, they got a little taste of the Bermuda Triangle when the instruments in their four-seater plane all went wacky and wiggled around. But they were able to make their way through the anomalous airspace without disappearing off the face of the earth. A pilot license opens up a world of possibilities and maybe a portal to another dimension.

Earning a pilot license is an exciting endeavor that requires dedication, commitment, and a passion for aviation.

There are different types of pilot licenses available, but I assume you would want the Private Pilot License (PPL). However, other common licenses include Commercial Pilot License (CPL), and Airline Transport Pilot License (ATPL). Determine whether you want to fly for recreational purposes, to pursue a career in aviation, or both.

To qualify for a pilot license, you must meet certain basic requirements set by aviation authorities such as the Federal Aviation Administration (FAA) in the United States or the Civil Aviation Authority (CAA) in other countries. Requirements typically include being at least 17 years old (for a PPL) and having a valid medical certificate issued by an aviation medical examiner.

Enroll in a reputable flight school or find a certified flight instructor (CFI) to guide you through the training process. Look for schools or instructors with experienced staff, modern training aircraft, and a comprehensive curriculum. Visit different schools, talk to instructors, and ask for recommendations from other pilots.

Start your pilot training by completing ground school, which covers essential topics, such as aerodynamics, aircraft systems, navigation, weather theory, regulations, and flight planning. Ground school can be completed through a formal classroom course, online training program, or self-study using textbooks and study guides.

Begin your flight training under the guidance of a qualified flight instructor. Flight training typically consists of dual instruction (flying with an instructor) and solo practice flights. You'll learn basic flight maneuvers, takeoffs, landings, navigation, emergency procedures, and other essential flying skills. Progress through a structured training syllabus designed to prepare you for the practical test.

Log flight hours and gain experience to meet the minimum flight time requirements for the pilot license you're pursuing. The exact requirements vary depending on the type of license and the regulations of the aviation authority in your country. Practice flying in different weather conditions, airspace environments, and types of aircraft to develop your skills and confidence as a pilot.

Study for and pass the written knowledge exam administered by the aviation authority in your country. The exam covers the topics learned in ground school and flight training and typically consists of multiple-choice questions. Use study guides, practice exams, and review materials to prepare for the exam.

Once you've completed the required flight training and logged the necessary flight hours, you'll need to pass a practical flight test (also known as a check ride) administered by a designated pilot examiner (DPE) or aviation authority inspector. During the check ride, you'll demonstrate your flying skills, knowledge, and ability to operate an aircraft safely and proficiently.

Upon successful completion of the written exam and practical flight test, you'll be issued a pilot license by the aviation authority in your country. Your license will indicate the type of pilot privileges and ratings you've earned, such as VFR (Visual Flight Rules) or IFR (Instrument Flight Rules) privileges, aircraft category, and class ratings, and any additional endorsements or restrictions.

Earning a pilot license is just the beginning of your journey as a pilot. Stay current with aviation regulations, safety practices, and emerging technologies. Pursue additional training, endorsements, or advanced ratings to expand your skills and qualifications as a pilot. Join aviation organizations, participate in flying clubs, and connect with other pilots to continue learning and growing in the aviation community.

Earning a pilot license is a challenging and rewarding accomplishment that opens up a world of opportunities for exploration, adventure, and personal fulfillment. With dedication, perseverance, and a commitment to safety, you can achieve your dream of becoming a pilot and enjoy the freedom of flight.

Earn a Scuba Diving Certification

Did you ever want to explore the bottom of a lake or swim among the fish along a beautiful coral reef? Earn a scuba diving certification, and you are on your way. It is an exciting and rewarding process that allows you to explore the underwater world safely.

There are several internationally recognized scuba diving certification agencies, including PADI (Professional Association of Diving Instructors), NAUI (National Association of Underwater Instructors), SSI (Scuba Schools International), and SDI/TDI (Scuba Diving International/Technical Diving International). Research these agencies to find one that offers courses in your area and aligns with your learning preferences.

Select a scuba diving certification course that fits your schedule, budget, and skill level. Most agencies offer beginner-level courses, such as the PADI Open Water Diver course or the NAUI Scuba Diver course, which are designed for individuals with little to no diving experience.

Enroll in the chosen scuba diving course, and begin the knowledge development portion of the training. This typically involves studying diving theory, safety procedures, equipment operation, and environmental considerations. You may complete this portion of the course through self-study using textbooks, online materials, or interactive e-learning platforms provided by the certification agency.

Participate in confined water training sessions, also known as pool or shallow water sessions, to learn essential scuba diving skills under the guidance of a certified instructor. Practice skills such as mask clearing, regulator recovery, buoyancy control, and underwater communication in a controlled environment before progressing to open water dives.

Once you've mastered the basic skills in confined water, complete a series of open water dives to apply what you've learned in real diving conditions. These dives typically take place in a natural body of water, such as a lake, quarry, or ocean under the supervision of your instructor. Demonstrate your ability to dive safely, navigate underwater, and respond to various diving scenarios.

Successfully complete a final written exam to demonstrate your understanding of diving theory, safety procedures, and equipment operation. The exam typically covers topics learned during the knowledge development portion of the course and may be administered online or in person.

Upon successful completion of the course requirements, you'll receive a scuba diving certification card from the certification agency. This card serves as proof that you've completed the necessary training and are qualified to scuba dive within the limits of your certification level. Your certification card will indicate the type of certification you've earned (e.g., PADI Open Water Diver, NAUI Scuba Diver) and any additional endorsements or specialties you may have completed.

Scuba diving is a lifelong learning journey, and there are many opportunities to further your diving education and skills. Consider enrolling in advanced-level courses, specialty courses (e.g., wreck diving, night diving, underwater photography), or technical diving courses to expand your knowledge and experience as a diver.

By following these steps and completing a scuba diving certification course, you'll gain the knowledge, skills, and confidence to explore the underwater world safely and responsibly. Enjoy the adventure of scuba diving and the wonders that await beneath the surface!

Earn a Wine Tasting Certification

Do you enjoy wine? Do you struggle to appreciate the differences between various wines? Do you wish you had a broader understanding of wines? Do you wish you could converse more intelligently about wines? Do you just wish you could select a wine you know you would enjoy from a row of bottles at a store? Why not indulge this vacuum in your life by taking it a little bit to the other extreme? Earning a wine tasting certification can be an enjoyable and educational journey for wine enthusiasts who want to deepen their knowledge and appreciation of wine.

Start by researching wine tasting certification programs to find one that aligns with your goals, interests, and level of expertise. Some of the most reputable wine certification programs include the Court of Master Sommeliers, the Wine & Spirit Education Trust (WSET), and the Society of Wine Educators. Each program offers different levels of certification, from beginner to advanced.

Decide which level of certification you want to pursue based on your current knowledge and experience with wine. Most certification programs offer multiple levels, such as introductory, intermediate, and advanced. If you're new to wine tasting, you may want to start with an introductory level course while more experienced tasters may opt for intermediate or advanced levels.

Enroll in a wine tasting certification course offered by a certified provider or accredited institution. Many programs offer both in-person and online courses to accommodate different learning preferences and schedules. Choose a course format that works best for you and fits your budget.

Participate in classes, tastings, and workshops as part of your certification course. Learn about wine production, grape varieties, winemaking techniques, wine regions, tasting terminology, and sensory evaluation methods. Practice tasting a wide variety of wines from different regions and styles to develop your palate and sensory skills.

Dedicate time to studying course materials, textbooks, and resources provided by the certification program. Review wine tasting notes, maps, and reference guides to familiarize yourself with key wine regions, grape varieties, and wine styles. Practice blind tasting exercises to improve your ability to identify wines based on taste, aroma, and appearance.

Take practice exams and quizzes to assess your knowledge and understanding of wine tasting concepts and terminology. Practice answering questions on wine theory, wine production, wine service, and wine styles to prepare for the certification exam.

Once you feel confident in your knowledge and skills, schedule the certification exam with the certification program. The exam may consist of multiple-choice questions, written essays, blind tasting assessments, and practical demonstrations of wine service and wine pairing. Make sure to review the exam format, content areas, and scoring criteria beforehand.

On the day of the exam, arrive early, well-rested, and prepared to demonstrate your knowledge and tasting abilities. Follow all instructions provided by the exam proctors, and adhere to the exam rules and regulations. Stay calm, focused, and confident throughout the exam.

Upon successful completion of the certification exam, you'll receive your wine tasting certification from the certification program. Your certification may include a formal certificate, a lapel pin, and a listing in the program's online database of certified professionals. Celebrate your achievement, and proudly display your certification credentials.

Wine tasting is a lifelong journey of discovery and enjoyment. Stay engaged with the wine community, attend tastings, events, and seminars, and continue to explore new wines and wine regions. Consider pursuing advanced-level certifications or specialization courses to further enhance your expertise and credibility as a wine taster.

By following these steps and dedicating time and effort to your wine tasting education, you'll earn a wine tasting certification and gain the knowledge, skills, and confidence to appreciate and enjoy wine at a deeper level. Cheers to your wine tasting journey!

Chapter 6
Exercise and Health

"I'm not just retiring from the company; I'm also retiring from my stress, my commute, my alarm clock, and my iron."

—Hartman Jule

Somewhat Unconventional

Here are some healthy and somewhat unconventional ideas that can add excitement and wellness to your life:

- **Urban Foraging**: Explore your city or town for edible wild plants and fruits. Learn about local flora and fauna while collecting nutritious ingredients for homemade meals.
- **Aerial Yoga**: Take aerial yoga classes, which combine traditional yoga poses with the use of aerial hammocks or silks. This unique form of yoga enhances flexibility, core strength, and relaxation.
- **Gardening Therapy**: Spend time tending to a garden, whether it's a small plot in your backyard or a community garden. Gardening is not only physically rewarding but also mentally calming and stress-relieving.
- **Tai Chi in Nature**: Practice Tai Chi in natural settings, such as parks or gardens. Tai Chi promotes balance, flexibility, and relaxation while connecting with the surrounding environment.
- **Geocaching Adventures**: Join the global treasure-hunting game of geocaching, where participants use GPS coordinates to find hidden containers or "geocaches" in outdoor locations. It's a fun way to stay active while exploring new areas.
- **Flotation Therapy**: Experience flotation therapy sessions in sensory deprivation tanks filled with Epsom salt water. Flotation therapy promotes relaxation, stress reduction, and mental clarity.

- **Laughter Yoga**: Join laughter yoga sessions where participants engage in playful exercises, deep breathing, and laughter to promote physical and emotional well-being.
- **Wild Swimming**: Take up the exhilarating activity of wild swimming in natural bodies of water, such as lakes, rivers, or oceans. Swimming in nature provides a refreshing workout while connecting with the environment.
- **Cold Water Immersion**: Embrace the health benefits of cold water immersion by taking cold showers or dips in cold water. Cold exposure boosts circulation, strengthens the immune system, and improves mood.
- **Barefoot Walking**: Practice barefoot walking on natural surfaces, such as grass, sand, or dirt, to strengthen the feet, improve balance, and connect with the earth.
- **Outdoor Meditation Retreats**: Attend outdoor meditation retreats held in natural settings, such as forests, mountains, or beaches. Outdoor meditation enhances mindfulness, relaxation, and spiritual connection with nature.
- **Forest Bathing**: Engage in the Japanese practice of forest bathing, or Shinrin-yoku, by immersing yourself in nature and mindfully connecting with the sights, sounds, and smells of the forest. Forest bathing reduces stress, boosts mood, and supports overall well-being.
- **Thermal Springs Soaking**: Visit natural thermal springs or hot springs for therapeutic soaking in mineral-rich waters. Thermal springs bathing promotes relaxation, relieves muscle tension, and supports detoxification.
- **Gong Bath Therapy**: Immerse yourself in the soothing sounds of gong bath therapy and receive deep relaxation and stress relief. Attend gong bath sessions or workshops to experience the healing vibrations of gongs and other sound instruments.
- **Solar Gazing**: Practice solar gazing, a meditation technique that involves gazing at the sun during safe times, such as sunrise or sunset. Solar gazing is believed to enhance energy levels, improve mood, and support overall health.

While solar gazing meditation may offer spiritual and psychological benefits for some individuals, it also carries potential risks and safety concerns. Staring directly at the sun, especially during peak hours when sunlight is intense, can cause eye damage, retinal burns, and vision impairment. It is essential to exercise caution and follow safety guidelines when practicing solar gazing meditation.

If you're interested in exploring solar gazing meditation, it's important to seek guidance from experienced practitioners or spiritual teachers who can provide instruction, support, and supervision. They can help you learn proper techniques, establish safe practices, and minimize the risk of eye injury or sun damage.

- **Breathwork Workshops**: Attend breathwork workshops or classes that teach deep breathing techniques, pranayama, or breath-focused meditation for relaxation and stress relief.
- **Holotropic Breathwork Retreats**: Attend holotropic breathwork retreats or workshops that use deep breathing techniques to induce altered states of consciousness and emotional healing. Holotropic breathwork promotes self-awareness and personal growth.
- **Hiking Meditation**: Combine hiking with mindfulness meditation by practicing walking meditation techniques while hiking on scenic trails. Hiking meditation promotes mental clarity, stress reduction, and connection with nature.
- **Naked Gardening**: Embrace the freedom of gardening in the nude, connecting with nature while cultivating plants and flowers. Naked gardening promotes body positivity, relaxation, and vitamin D absorption. However, you might want to make sure you have a very tall fence around your garden or around your yard.
- **Silent Retreats**: Participate in silent retreats where participants observe periods of silence while engaging in meditation, yoga, and mindfulness practices. Silent retreats promote inner peace, clarity, and spiritual growth.

- **Biohacking Experiments**: Explore biohacking techniques, such as cold exposure, intermittent fasting, and light therapy to optimize physical and mental performance. Biohacking promotes longevity, vitality, and well-being.
- **Skydiving Adventures**: Experience the thrill of skydiving by taking tandem jumps with experienced instructors. Skydiving boosts adrenaline, confidence, and a sense of accomplishment.

My wife was in a jump club in her younger years and racked up 23 jumps. She even did two formation jumps. This was back in the days when they did not do tandem jumps. She was part of a group that hung out together and jumped together. It was a tight community.

Nobody in her group died. In fact, no one was even injured. Though she did get lost for a while once when she got off course a bit and landed in a cornfield that was much taller than she is. But she climbed partway up a telephone pole, was able to get her bearings, and walked to a road. There were no cell phones in those days, but her friends watched where she landed, and they were able to cruise the nearby roads until they found her.

On another occasion, one of her friends landed in a farmer's field that had a bull in it. But this was no ordinary field. No. This was a magic field, and the bull was put there to protect it. Next, the most extraordinary thing happened. As he was running, he noticed that all of the parachuting gear he was carrying became much, much lighter and his legs moved much faster. Due to the powers of that charmed field, lickety-split, he was able to make it over the fence before the bull caught up to him. Sadly, after he cleared the fence, the spell was broken and he was just a mortal once again.

You may question the sanity of all this, but she assures me this sport is quite fun.

These healthy and somewhat unconventional ideas can help you stay active, improve your well-being, and explore new experiences. Whether you're interested in outdoor adventures, holistic wellness practices, or unique fitness activities, there's something for everyone to enjoy and benefit from.

For the Extremely Fit

Here are some fun activities you should try only if you are extremely fit. Most of these are more intense than older individuals should attempt. But if you are very fit and limber, these can offer you interesting challenges.

- **Rock Climbing Adventures**: Explore outdoor climbing spots or indoor climbing gyms. It's a full-body workout that improves strength, flexibility, and mental focus.
- **Indoor Trampoline Parks**: Visit indoor trampoline parks for a fun and energizing workout. Jumping on trampolines improves cardiovascular health, coordination, and mood in a playful and social environment.
- **Parkour Training**: Learn the art of parkour, a discipline that involves moving efficiently through urban environments by overcoming obstacles with running, jumping, and climbing techniques. Parkour enhances agility, strength, and mental focus. Parkour builds coordination and spatial awareness.
- **Wilderness Survival Skills**: Attend wilderness survival workshops or courses to learn essential skills, such as fire-making, shelter-building, and foraging. It's a fun and educational way to connect with nature and build self-reliance.
- **Stand-Up Paddleboard Yoga**: Try stand-up paddleboard (SUP) yoga, a unique form of yoga practiced on a paddleboard in calm water. SUP yoga improves balance, core strength, and mindfulness.
- **Outdoor Trampoline Fitness**: Invest in a high-quality outdoor trampoline, and engage in fun and low-impact exercises like bouncing, jogging, and jumping. It's a great way to improve cardiovascular health and balance while having fun.

Trampoline workouts are excellent for cardiovascular health and coordination.

- **Aerial Silks Training**: Learn aerial silks or aerial fabric techniques where you perform acrobatic movements on suspended silks. Aerial silks training improves strength, flexibility, and gracefulness.
- **AcroYoga Workshops**: Attend AcroYoga workshops that combine acrobatics, yoga, and Thai massage. AcroYoga builds trust, communication, and physical fitness in a supportive and playful environment.
- **Mountain Unicycling**: Master the skill of mountain unicycling (MUNI), where you ride a unicycle on rugged terrain such as mountain trails. Mountain unicycling improves balance, coordination, and cardiovascular fitness.
- **Animal Flow Workouts**: Practice animal flow workouts inspired by animal movements, such as crawling, jumping, and rolling. Animal flow enhances mobility, strength, and agility in a dynamic and playful way.
- **Fire Dancing Performances**: Learn fire dancing techniques, such as poi spinning, staff twirling, or fire hooping. Fire dancing combines dance, rhythm, and flow arts for a mesmerizing and exhilarating performance.
- **Breath-Hold Diving Training**: Train in breath-hold diving techniques to explore the underwater world without scuba gear. Breath-hold diving improves lung capacity, relaxation, and aquatic exploration skills.
- **Horseback Archery**: Horseback archery combines archery with horse riding skills. It requires riders to shoot arrows at targets while riding at various speeds. It's a thrilling and adventurous sport that connects people with nature and history.
- **Bossaball**: Bossaball is a hybrid sport that combines elements of volleyball, soccer, gymnastics, and capoeira. It's played on an inflatable court with trampolines on each side, allowing players to perform acrobatic jumps and spikes.
- **Slacklining**: Slacklining involves walking or balancing on a flat, stretchy band suspended between two anchor points. It's a

challenging and meditative activity that improves balance, core strength, and focus.

These healthy and unusual activities offer opportunities to explore new experiences, challenge yourself physically and mentally, and enhance your overall well-being. Whether you're interested in outdoor adventures, alternative therapies, or creative pursuits, these offer you the opportunity to try something new.

For Just About Anyone

Here are some healthy ideas to help you stay active, engaged, and in good health:

- **Regular Exercise Routine**: Develop a consistent exercise routine that includes a mix of cardiovascular activities, strength training, and flexibility exercises.
- **Daily Walking**: Make walking a daily habit by taking brisk walks around your neighborhood, local parks, or nature trails. Aim for at least 30 minutes of walking each day.
- **Yoga Practice**: Start a regular yoga practice to improve flexibility, balance, and strength while reducing stress and promoting relaxation.
- **Swimming**: Take up swimming as a low-impact exercise that works out the entire body and improves cardiovascular health.
- **Cycling**: Enjoy the benefits of cycling by riding a bike outdoors or using a stationary bike indoors. Cycling is great for cardiovascular fitness and leg strength.
- **Healthy Eating Habits**: Adopt a balanced and nutritious diet. There is a huge debate right now about what constitutes a healthy diet. Many sources now advocate removing all carbohydrates and sugar from our diet. This is often called a keto diet. I believe everyone should decide for themselves what they believe is healthy. To do this, you need to research the topic. I personally have found topics discussed on Dr. Ken Berry's YouTube channel to be extremely helpful. Everyone should explore and make up their own mind.

- **Mindful Eating**: Practice mindful eating by paying attention to your food choices, savoring each bite, and eating slowly to better regulate appetite and enjoy meals.
- **Regular Health Check-ups**: Schedule regular check-ups with your healthcare provider for preventive screenings, vaccinations, and health assessments. I have friends and relatives who died suddenly in their 50s, and I have to think this might have been avoided in many cases had they seen a doctor annually for a check-up. But, again, I believe everyone should research health topics for themselves. I know that doctors do the best they can with the information available to them. I also know they have certain constraints imposed upon them by their profession. They are also extremely busy and cannot possibly digest all of the new information being generated these days.

  You have the most to lose by surrendering your decision to other individuals without questioning those decisions or become being better informed yourself. I know the information can be daunting and overwhelming. But start by researching just one thing at a time. And do get a regular check-up.
- **Stay Hydrated**: Drink plenty of water throughout the day to stay hydrated and support overall health, digestion, and cognitive function.
- **Strength Training**: Incorporate strength training exercises into your routine to build muscle mass, improve bone density, and enhance metabolism.
- **Healthy Sleep Habits**: Prioritize getting enough sleep each night by establishing a consistent sleep schedule, creating a relaxing bedtime routine, and optimizing your sleep environment.
- **Mental Stimulation**: Keep your mind sharp and engaged by pursuing hobbies, learning new skills, reading books, or solving puzzles and brain teasers.
- **Social Connections**: Maintain strong social connections by spending time with family and friends, joining clubs or social groups, and participating in community activities.

- **Mindfulness Meditation**: Practice mindfulness meditation to reduce stress, improve focus and attention, and cultivate a greater sense of inner peace and well-being.
- **Healthy Cooking**: Experiment with healthy cooking techniques and recipes at home to prepare delicious and nutritious meals using fresh, whole ingredients.
- **Stress Management**: Manage stress effectively through relaxation techniques, such as deep breathing exercises, progressive muscle relaxation, or meditation.
- **Outdoor Activities**: Spend time outdoors enjoying activities like gardening, hiking, birdwatching, or nature photography to connect with nature and promote physical and mental health.
- **Cognitive Exercises**: Challenge your brain with cognitive exercises, such as crossword puzzles, Sudoku, memory games, or learning a new language to maintain cognitive function and mental acuity.
- **Gratitude Practice**: Cultivate an attitude of gratitude by reflecting on the positive aspects of your life, expressing appreciation for the people and experiences around you, and keeping a gratitude journal.

By incorporating these healthy ideas into your lifestyle, you can prioritize your physical and mental well-being, stay active and engaged, and make the most of your retirement years.

A Little Running Around

Here are some unique sport ideas to keep you active, engaged, and having fun:

- **Pickleball**: A combination of tennis, badminton, and ping-pong, pickleball is played with a paddle and a plastic ball on a smaller court. It's easy to learn and is great for all skill levels.
- **Bocce Ball**: A traditional Italian game, bocce involves throwing balls toward a target ball (pallino) on a designated court. It's a social and strategic game that can be played competitively or casually.

- **Disc Golf**: Similar to traditional golf, disc golf involves throwing flying discs into metal baskets instead of hitting balls into holes. It's a fun and challenging outdoor activity that combines athleticism and strategy.
- **Frisbee Freestyle**: Freestyle frisbee involves performing tricks and maneuvers with a frisbee, such as spinning, throwing, and catching. It's a creative and dynamic sport that's fun to practice alone or with others.
- **Archery Tag**: Archery tag combines archery with elements of dodgeball and paintball. Players use bows and foam-tipped arrows to tag opponents and score points while avoiding being hit themselves.
- **Ultimate Frisbee**: Ultimate frisbee is a fast-paced team sport played with a flying disc. Players pass the disc to teammates and score points by catching it in the opposing team's end zone. It's a great way to stay active and socialize with others.
- **Racquetball**: Racquetball is a fast-paced indoor sport played with a small rubber ball and racquets on a walled court. It's a great cardiovascular workout and can be played at various skill levels.
- **Spikeball**: Spikeball is a fun and fast-paced game played with a small trampoline-like net and a ball. Players bounce the ball off the net and try to prevent their opponents from returning it. It's easy to learn and can be played virtually anywhere.
- **Synchronized Swimming**: Synchronized swimming is a graceful and synchronized team sport performed in water that combines elements of swimming, dance, and gymnastics. It's a great way to improve strength, flexibility, and coordination while expressing creativity and teamwork.
- **Quidditch**: Inspired by the fictional sport from the Harry Potter series, quidditch is a real-life game played on broomsticks that combines elements of rugby, dodgeball, and tag. Players aim to score points by throwing balls through hoops while avoiding being hit by bludgers.
- **Cyclocross**: Cyclocross is a form of bicycle racing that takes place on off-road courses with obstacles, such as mud, sand,

and barriers. It's a challenging and adrenaline-pumping sport that combines cycling skills with running and jumping.

- **Tchoukball**: Tchoukball is a team sport played with a small ball and rebound surfaces at each end of the court. Players score points by throwing the ball at the rebound surfaces in a way that prevents the opposing team from catching it.
- **Kin-Ball**: Kin-Ball is a cooperative team sport played with a large inflatable ball and three teams on a circular court. Players work together to prevent the ball from touching the ground while trying to score points by hitting it toward the opposing teams.
- **Bubble Soccer**: Bubble soccer, also known as bubble football, is a hilarious and entertaining sport where players wear inflatable bubbles and try to play soccer while bumping into each other. It's a great way to have fun and get some exercise with friends and family.

These unique sport ideas for retirement offer a wide range of options for staying active, socializing with others, and exploring new interests and challenges. Whether you prefer individual activities or team sports, there's something for everyone to enjoy and stay healthy in retirement.

A Lot of Running Around

If you really enjoy running, here are some outdoor running ideas to keep you active and exploring:

- **Scenic Trail Runs**: Discover nearby hiking trails and nature reserves for scenic trail runs surrounded by natural beauty.
- **Park Runs**: Explore local parks and green spaces for leisurely runs amidst lush landscapes, playgrounds, and picnic areas.
- **Beach Runs**: Enjoy salty breezes and the sound of crashing waves with invigorating runs along sandy shores.
- **Urban Runs**: Explore your city's streets, neighborhoods, and landmarks on urban runs, and discover hidden gems and architectural marvels along the way.

- **Historic Runs**: Combine fitness and history by running through historic districts, visiting landmarks, monuments, and heritage sites.
- **River Runs**: Follow riverside paths and waterfront promenades for tranquil runs with scenic views of flowing water and lush vegetation.
- **Mountain Runs**: Challenge yourself with mountain runs on rugged trails and steep inclines, and be rewarded with breathtaking panoramic views at the summit.
- **Lake Runs**: Circumnavigate picturesque lakes or reservoirs for peaceful runs with serene water views and abundant wildlife.
- **Country Road Runs**: Explore rural landscapes and countryside vistas on quiet country roads, and enjoy fresh air and wide-open spaces.
- **Farm Runs**: Visit local farms and orchards for scenic runs through rolling fields, pastures, and orchards with opportunities to sample fresh produce along the way.
- **Vineyard Runs**: Run through vineyards and wine country, soak in scenic vineyard views, and taste local wines at wineries along the route.
- **Waterfall Runs**: Seek out trails that lead to cascading waterfalls for refreshing runs with the soothing sound of rushing water.
- **Botanical Garden Runs**: Enjoy runs through botanical gardens and arboretums, surrounded by colorful blooms, fragrant flowers, and lush foliage.
- **Wildlife Runs**: Explore nature reserves and wildlife sanctuaries for runs amidst diverse ecosystems, and spot birds, mammals, and other wildlife along the way.
- **Coastal Runs**: Run along coastal cliffs, bluffs, or boardwalks for exhilarating runs with sweeping ocean views and sea breezes.
- **Canyon Runs**: Embark on runs through scenic canyons and gorges, and marvel at towering rock formations and dramatic landscapes.
- **Staircase Runs**: Incorporate staircases and stairwells into your runs for intense cardio workouts and leg strength training.

- **Botanical Trail Runs**: Discover botanical trails and interpretive nature walks for educational runs with informative signage and themed gardens.
- **Alpine Runs**: Escape to high-altitude destinations for alpine runs amidst alpine meadows, glacial lakes, and snow-capped peaks with crisp mountain air and stunning vistas.

These outdoor running ideas offer a variety of experiences to keep you motivated, engaged, and inspired as you explore new routes, terrains, and destinations. Whether you prefer serene nature trails, urban adventures, or scenic vistas, there's something for every runner to enjoy.

See More of the Outdoors

Here are some fun outdoor ideas to help you stay active, engaged, and enjoy the great outdoors:

- **Picnic in the Park**: Pack a picnic basket with your favorite snacks and head to a nearby park for a relaxing outdoor meal with friends or family.
- **Nature Photography**: Explore local parks, nature reserves, and scenic landscapes with a camera in hand, and capture the beauty of nature through photography.
- **Outdoor Yoga**: Practice yoga in the fresh air by attending outdoor yoga classes or simply rolling out a mat in your backyard or a nearby park.
- **Birdwatching**: Grab a pair of binoculars and a field guide and go birdwatching in natural habitats, such as wetlands, forests, or coastal areas.
- **Kayaking or Canoeing**: Paddle along rivers, lakes, or coastal waterways by renting kayaks or canoes for a leisurely and scenic outdoor adventure.
- **Fishing**: Spend a day fishing at a local lake, pond, or river, and enjoy the tranquility of nature while trying to reel in a big catch.
- **Cycling**: Explore bike trails, scenic routes, or urban streets by going for leisurely bike rides or joining group cycling events in your community.

- **Outdoor Cooking**: Host a barbecue or cookout in your backyard, and grill up delicious burgers, hot dogs, and veggies for friends and family to enjoy.
- **Botanical Garden Visits**: Visit botanical gardens or arboretums to admire colorful flowers, exotic plants, and themed gardens while soaking in the beauty of nature.
- **Outdoor Concerts**: Attend outdoor concerts or music festivals held in parks, amphitheaters, or open-air venues, and enjoy live music performances in a scenic setting.
- **Stargazing**: Set up a telescope or simply lay out a blanket and gaze at the stars on clear nights, identify constellations, and marvel at the beauty of the night sky.
- **Outdoor Movie Nights**: Host outdoor movie nights in your backyard or community park. Project films onto a screen or hang a white sheet for a makeshift theater experience.
- **Wildlife Safari**: Go on wildlife safaris to observe animals in their natural habitats, whether it's birdwatching, whale watching, or taking a safari tour in a national park.
- **Nature Walks**: Take leisurely walks or guided nature hikes along scenic trails. Learn about local flora, fauna, and ecosystems while getting exercise outdoors.
- **Outdoor Games**: Organize outdoor games and sports activities, such as volleyball, frisbee, badminton, or cornhole tournaments, for friendly competition and fun.
- **Botanical Crafting**: Gather natural materials, such as leaves, flowers, and branches, to create botanical crafts like flower crowns, leaf rubbings, or pressed flower art.
- **Outdoor Art**: Set up an easel and paint outdoors, and capture scenic landscapes, cityscapes, or still life compositions en plein air.
- **Outdoor Fitness Classes**: Join outdoor fitness classes, such as boot camps, yoga sessions, or tai chi classes, held in parks or open spaces for a fun and invigorating workout experience.

These fun, outdoor ideas for retirement offer a wide range of activities to enjoy the beauty of nature, stay active, and create lasting memories with loved ones. Whether you prefer relaxing picnics, adventurous outings, or cultural experiences, there's something for everyone to enjoy outdoors.

Activities in the Winter

Here are some fun winter ideas for retirement to keep you active, entertained, and enjoying the season:

- **Skiing or Snowboarding**: Hit the slopes at a nearby ski resort for downhill skiing or snowboarding adventures, and enjoy the thrill of speeding down snowy mountainsides.
- **Snowshoeing**: Explore scenic trails and winter landscapes by snowshoeing through snowy forests, parks, or on mountain trails at your own pace.
- **Curling**: Curling is a winter sport played on ice where players slide stones toward a target area while teammates sweep the ice to control the stone's speed and direction. It's a strategic and social sport that's accessible to people of all ages.
- **Ice Skating**: Lace up your skates and glide across outdoor ice rinks or frozen lakes. Enjoy the classic winter activity with friends and family.
- **Winter Hiking**: Bundle up and go for winter hikes along snowy trails. Admire snow-covered scenery and spot wildlife in tranquil natural settings.
- **Snow Tubing**: Have fun zooming down snow-covered hills on inflatable snow tubes at tubing parks or designated snow tubing slopes.
- **Cross-Country Skiing**: Enjoy the serenity of cross-country skiing on groomed trails or in backcountry areas as you explore winter wonderlands at a slower pace.
- **Ice Fishing**: Bundle up and head to frozen lakes or ponds for ice fishing adventures. Drill holes in the ice and try to catch fish beneath the frozen surface.
- **Winter Camping**: Embrace the beauty of winter by camping in snow-covered landscapes, either in tents or cozy cabins, and enjoying activities like snowshoeing and campfires.

- **Winter Birdwatching**: Bundle up and go birdwatching in winter, and observe migratory birds, waterfowl, and other winter residents in their natural habitats.
- **Hot Springs Soaking**: Relax and unwind in natural hot springs or hot tubs by soaking in warm water while surrounded by snowy scenery.
- **Winter Photography**: Capture the beauty of winter landscapes with photography outings, taking photos of snow-covered trees, icy lakes, and frosty landscapes.
- **Winter Festivals**: Attend winter festivals and events in your community or nearby towns, and enjoy activities like ice sculpting, snow carving, and winter parades.
- **Winter Carnivals**: Participate in winter carnivals featuring snow games, ice skating, sleigh rides, and other festive activities for all ages.
- **Sleigh Rides**: Enjoy the nostalgia of bundling up in blankets and taking horse-drawn sleigh rides through snowy fields or forested trails while savoring the winter scenery.
- **Indoor Crafts**: Stay cozy indoors and explore creative hobbies, such as knitting, quilting, painting, or crafting. Make handmade gifts or home decor.
- **Winter Gardening**: Plan and prepare for spring by engaging in indoor gardening activities, such as seed starting, plant propagation, and tending to houseplants.
- **Cooking and Baking**: Experiment with winter recipes and baking projects. Try your hand at making comfort foods, soups, stews, and seasonal treats.
- **Winter Reading**: Curl up with a good book or join a book club to explore new literary worlds and stay entertained during chilly winter days and nights.
- **Volunteer Work**: Give back to your community by volunteering for winter-related activities, such as food drives, coat donations, or helping those in need during the cold season.

These fun winter ideas for retirement offer a variety of activities to enjoy the season, whether you prefer outdoor adventures in the snow, cozy indoor hobbies, or community events and festivities. Embrace the spirit of winter and make the most of the season with activities that bring joy, relaxation, and fulfillment in retirement.

A Lot to Do at the Beach

Here are some fun things you can do at the beach. If you live close to a beach or visit a beach, consider giving some of these a try. These can help you make the most of your time by the sea:

- **Beach Picnics**: Pack a basket with your favorite snacks and beverages, and enjoy a picnic on a sandy shore with family and friends.
- **Sandcastle Building**: Channel your inner child and build elaborate sandcastles or sculptures with buckets, shovels, and molds.
- **Beach Volleyball**: Set up a beach volleyball net and enjoy a friendly game with friends or join a pickup game with fellow beachgoers.
- **Sunbathing and Relaxing**: Soak up the sun's rays on a comfortable beach towel or lounge chair while listening to the sound of waves crashing nearby.
- **Swimming and Snorkeling**: Take a refreshing dip in the ocean and explore underwater marine life by snorkeling in clear, shallow waters.
- **Beachcombing**: Walk along the shoreline and search for seashells, sand dollars, and other treasures washed ashore by the tide.
- **Bodyboarding or Surfing**: Ride the waves on a bodyboard or surfboard, catch waves, and experience the thrill of surfing.
- **Beach Yoga**: Practice yoga on the beach by combining gentle stretches, poses, and breathing exercises with the calming sounds of the ocean.
- **Beach Bonfires**: Gather around a beach bonfire with friends and family in the evening, roast marshmallows, tell stories, and enjoy the warmth of the fire.

- **Beach Bonfire Movie Nights**: Host movie nights on the beach by setting up a large screen and projector near a bonfire, allowing everyone to enjoy outdoor cinema under the stars.
- **Beachside Bonfire Cooking Classes:** Attend cooking classes or workshops held around beach bonfires, and learn how to prepare delicious meals using campfire cooking techniques and local ingredients.
- **Beach Barbecues**: Grill delicious meals on portable barbecue grills or fire pits set up on the beach, and enjoy outdoor dining with ocean views.
- **Beach Games**: Play classic beach games, like frisbee, paddleball, beach bocce, or beach cricket, for hours of fun in the sun.
- **Beach Photography**: Capture stunning beach scenes, sunsets, and seascapes with your camera or smartphone, and experiment with different angles and perspectives.
- **Underwater Photography**: Explore underwater photography by snorkeling or diving with a waterproof camera, and capture photos of the vibrant marine life and coral reefs beneath the surface.
- **Beach Fishing**: Cast a line and try your luck at beach fishing to catch fish, such as surfperch, halibut, or striped bass, from the shoreline.
- **Beach Cycling**: Explore coastal bike paths or ride along scenic beachfront roads on bicycles, and enjoy the sea breeze and ocean views.
- **Beach Kayaking**: Rent a kayak and paddle along the coastline, exploring hidden coves, rocky cliffs, and sea caves along the way.
- **Beachcomber Art**: Get creative with beachcomber art by arranging seashells, driftwood, and other beach finds into sculptures or mosaics on the sand.
- **Sand Art Competitions**: Organize or participate in sand art competitions where individuals or teams create intricate sculptures or designs using only sand and water.
- **Beachside Art Installations**: Create temporary art installations using natural materials found on the beach, such

as driftwood, shells, and seaweed, to express your creativity and connect with nature.

- **Beachside Art Therapy Workshops**: Participate in art therapy workshops held on the beach that use creative expression and artistic techniques to promote relaxation, self-discovery, and healing.
- **Beachside Dining**: Enjoy waterfront dining at beachside restaurants or cafes, and savor fresh seafood and tropical cocktails along with panoramic ocean views.
- **Beachside Spa Day**: Indulge in a relaxing spa day by booking beachside massages, facials, or yoga sessions offered by local resorts or wellness centers.
- **Beachside Yoga Retreats**: Join beachside yoga retreats or wellness workshops held at coastal resorts or retreat centers, combining yoga practice with relaxation and rejuvenation.
- **Beachside Yoga on Paddleboards**: Try the unique experience of practicing yoga on a paddleboard, combining the tranquility of yoga with the challenge of balancing on water.
- **Beachside Yoga and Surf Retreats**: Combine yoga practice with surfing lessons by joining yoga and surf retreats held at beachfront resorts or surf camps.
- **Beach Meditation Retreats**: Join beach meditation retreats or workshops where you can practice mindfulness and meditation techniques while listening to the soothing sounds of the waves.
- **Beach Conservation Activities**: Participate in beach cleanup events or volunteer for coastal conservation projects to help protect and preserve the natural beauty of the beach for future generations.
- **Sunset Drum Circles**: Gather with fellow beachgoers during sunset to participate in drum circles, creating rhythmic beats and music while enjoying the stunning views of the setting sun.
- **Beachside Drumming Workshops**: Participate in drumming workshops or classes held on the beach, and learn rhythmic patterns and techniques from experienced drummers.

- **Kite Surfing**: Try the exhilarating sport of kite surfing, where you harness the power of the wind to glide across the water while holding onto a kite.
- **Beachside Astronomy**: Set up telescopes on the beach for stargazing sessions that offer opportunities to observe celestial phenomena, such as meteor showers, planets, and constellations.
- **Beachside Astronomy Nights:** Attend astronomy nights or stargazing events held on the beach featuring telescope viewings, guided sky tours, and educational talks about astronomy.
- **Beachside Wildlife Safaris**: Join guided wildlife safaris or eco-tours along coastal habitats, and observe diverse wildlife, such as seabirds, dolphins, seals, and sea turtles, in their natural environment.
- **Beachside Wine Tastings**: Attend wine tastings or vineyard tours held at coastal wineries and sample a variety of wines while enjoying panoramic ocean views.
- **Beachside Outdoor Libraries**: Set up outdoor libraries or book exchanges on the beach that allow beachgoers to borrow or exchange books while they enjoy the seaside.
- **Beachside Tai Chi Classes**: Join Tai Chi classes or workshops held on the beach, and practice gentle movements and meditation techniques to improve balance, flexibility, and relaxation.
- **Beachside Sand Dune Sledding:** Experience the thrill of sand dune sledding by riding down sandy slopes on specially designed sand sleds or boards.
- **Beach Treasure Hunts**: Organize or participate in beach treasure hunts where participants search for hidden treasures buried in the sand, such as coins, trinkets, or message bottles.
- **Metal Detecting on the Beach**: Metal detecting on the beach offers a unique blend of excitement, adventure, and discovery for enthusiasts of all ages. Some enthusiasts even get detectors that can be submerged. Then, they search in the surf, and sometimes snorkel, to find submerged treasures. Whether you're searching for lost treasures, uncovering relics from the

past, or simply enjoying the beauty of the beach, beach metal detecting provides endless opportunities for exploration, enrichment, and enjoyment.

These fun beach ideas offer a variety of activities to enjoy the sun, sand, and surf while creating cherished memories and embracing the coastal lifestyle. Whether you're interested in creative arts, outdoor adventures, wellness activities, exploring coastal attractions, or just relaxing on the beach, there's something for everyone to enjoy by the sea.

Chapter 7
Spirituality

"Spirituality is basically our relationship with reality."

—Chandra Patel

Spirituality exploration can be a deeply personal and enriching journey that involves connecting with one's inner self, exploring existential questions, and seeking meaning and purpose in life. Seek truth. So often, people seek what they want to find and ignore what they don't want to see. They may even attack what they don't want to hear. But the truth remains, even if everyone denies it. The truth may be uncomfortable. To confuse the issue, people have created many beliefs. But there is power in the truth. It will help you grow.

Seek teachers who speak the truth plainly. If someone is not explaining their point plainly, then it probably does not contain the truth. I have my own beliefs that I feel very strongly about and feel that I am grounded in them. But I believe that everyone who honestly searches for the truth will find their way to pretty much the same destination.

Look at all of the equations physicists have been able to define to explain the orbits and physical properties of the things around us. No matter who discovers the formula or rediscovers the formula, they all find the same formula. That's because the formula is true. We need to have faith that our honest search for the truth will lead us where we need to go. We should also have the wisdom to realize there will be people who will try to hide the truth from us and try to trip us up.

People that speak gibberish may be well-meaning or perhaps they just want followers. But when you hear the truth, it is plain. It is in your face. It is like a light inside you turns on and you see further than you did before.

Meditation and Mindfulness

Practicing meditation and mindfulness techniques can help individuals cultivate inner peace, clarity, and awareness. Meditation involves quieting the mind, focusing on the present moment, and observing thoughts and sensations without judgment. Regular meditation practice can deepen spiritual connections, reduce stress, and foster a sense of inner calm and balance.

Reflection and Journaling

Taking time for self-reflection and journaling allows individuals to explore their thoughts, feelings, and beliefs in a structured and introspective manner. Writing about personal experiences, values, aspirations, and challenges can provide insights into one's spiritual journey and facilitate deeper self-understanding.

Nature Connection

Spending time in nature and immersing oneself in the natural world can be a powerful way to connect with spirituality. Whether it's taking walks in the forest, sitting by the ocean, or admiring the beauty of a sunset, nature offers opportunities for contemplation, awe, and reverence for the interconnectedness of all life.

Exploration of Sacred Texts and Wisdom Traditions

Studying sacred texts, scriptures, and wisdom from various spiritual and religious traditions can provide inspiration, guidance, and insights into the human experience and the nature of existence. Exploring different philosophies, beliefs, and teachings can broaden one's perspective and deepen spiritual understanding.

Prayer and Ritual

Engaging in prayer, rituals, and ceremonial practices can be a meaningful way to connect with the divine, express gratitude, and cultivate a sense of reverence and awe. Rituals can include lighting candles, offering prayers, chanting, or participating in communal ceremonies that honor spiritual principles and values.

Mind-Body Practices

Incorporating mind-body practices, such as yoga, tai chi, qigong, or energy healing techniques, into one's routine can promote holistic well-being and spiritual growth. These practices combine movement, breathwork, and mindfulness to harmonize the body, mind, and spirit, fostering a sense of balance and vitality.

Community and Fellowship

Joining spiritual communities, attending religious services, or participating in spiritual gatherings and retreats can provide opportunities for connection, support, and shared exploration of spirituality. Being part of a community of like-minded individuals can offer encouragement, inspiration, and a sense of belonging on the spiritual path.

Service and Compassion

Practicing acts of service, kindness, and compassion toward others can be a profound expression of spirituality. Volunteering, supporting charitable causes, and engaging in altruistic activities can cultivate empathy, generosity, and a sense of interconnectedness with all beings, fostering spiritual growth and fulfillment.

Creative Expression

Exploring creative outlets such as art, music, dance, writing, or storytelling can be a powerful way to express and explore spirituality. Creative expression allows individuals to tap into their innermost thoughts, emotions, and inspirations, transcending ordinary consciousness and connecting with deeper aspects of self and the universe.

Seeking Guidance and Mentorship

Seeking guidance from spiritual teachers, mentors, or counselors can provide support, wisdom, and perspective on one's spiritual journey. Mentors and spiritual guides can offer insights, tools, and practices to navigate challenges, deepen spiritual understanding, and cultivate a meaningful and fulfilling life aligned with one's highest aspirations.

Spirituality exploration is a deeply personal and multifaceted journey that invites you to explore your inner landscapes, connect with the divine, and discover meaning and purpose in life. In retirement, you have time to explore spirituality. You are off the treadmill and can take a hard, long look at the deep questions of life. By engaging in practices that resonate with your heart and soul, you can cultivate greater awareness, presence, and spiritual fulfillment on your unique path of exploration and discovery.

Chapter 8
Travel Near and Far

"Is there anything as horrible as starting on a trip? Once you're off, that's all right, but the last moments are earthquake and convulsion and the feeling that you are a snail being pulled off your rock."

—Anne Morrow Lindbergh

I must apologize for that quote, but it describes me, and I think there might be a few others that feel similarly. However, I know there are lots of people who love to travel, and it is very exciting to them. But for those that are like snails on a rock, this is the perfect time to widen your horizons. Venture out and see new places! This chapter is for everyone.

Travel and exploration in retirement offer a wealth of opportunities for fun, adventure, and discovery. There are many different types of travel experiences to choose from:

- **Bucket List Destinations**: Retirement is the perfect time to check off those bucket list destinations you've always dreamed of visiting. Whether it's exploring ancient ruins in Machu Picchu, cruising the fjords of Norway, or experiencing the vibrant culture of Tokyo, now is the time to make those dreams a reality. We already covered these in chapter one. You can refer to that section for more detail.
- **Slow Travel**: Retirement allows for a more relaxed pace of travel, so take advantage of this by embracing the concept of slow travel. Spend longer periods of time in each destination to allow yourself to become fully immersed in the local culture, cuisine, and way of life.
- **Off-the-Beaten-Path Adventures**: Venture off the beaten path and explore destinations that are less touristy but equally rewarding. Whether it's hiking remote trails in Patagonia, exploring hidden villages in rural France, or discovering hidden

gems in your own backyard, there's no shortage of off-the-beaten-path adventures to be had.

- **Cultural Immersion**: Use your retirement to dive deep into the local culture of the places you visit. Learn a new language, participate in cultural festivals and events, take cooking classes, or volunteer with local organizations to truly immerse yourself in the culture and customs of each destination.
- **Multigenerational Travel**: Retirement is a great time to travel with family and friends, including children and grandchildren. Create lasting memories by planning multigenerational trips that cater to everyone's interests and preferences.
- **Adventure Travel**: If you're an adrenaline junkie, retirement offers the perfect opportunity to indulge in adventure travel experiences. Whether it's skydiving over the Great Barrier Reef, whitewater rafting in the Grand Canyon, or trekking to Everest Base Camp, there are adventures to be found all around the world.
- **Culinary Experiences**: Food is an integral part of travel, so use your retirement to indulge in culinary experiences around the world. Whether it's sampling street food in Bangkok, indulging in wine and cheese in Tuscany, or taking a cooking class in Marrakech, there are delicious experiences in almost any destination you choose.
- **Cruise Travel**: Cruises offer a convenient and comfortable way to see multiple destinations in one trip. Whether you're cruising through the Caribbean, exploring the Mediterranean, or navigating the rivers of Europe, there's a cruise itinerary to suit every taste and interest.
- **Road Trips**: Hit the open road and embark on a classic road trip adventure. Whether it's driving along the iconic Route 66, exploring the scenic beauty of the Pacific Coast Highway, or navigating the rugged landscapes of the Australian Outback, road trips offer the freedom to explore at your own pace and discover hidden gems along the way.
- **Cultural Heritage Tours**: Explore the rich history and heritage of different cultures by taking cultural heritage tours. Whether it's tracing your ancestry through genealogy tours, visiting

118

UNESCO World Heritage sites, or exploring historical landmarks and museums, there are opportunities to learn about history and heritage in many places you visit.

Overall, retirement offers the perfect opportunity to indulge in travel and exploration, whether it's ticking off bucket list destinations, immersing yourself in local culture, or embarking on off-the-beaten-path adventures. Whatever your interests and preferences, there's a world of experiences waiting to be discovered in retirement travel.

Slow Travel

Slow travel options involve adopting a more leisurely and immersive approach to exploring destinations, emphasizing deeper connections with local culture, people, and landscapes. Here are several slow travel options:

- **Train Journeys**: Embark on scenic train journeys that offer a relaxed and scenic way to travel between destinations. Enjoy panoramic views of landscapes, picturesque villages, and historic landmarks while experiencing the rhythm of the rails. Train travel allows for a slower pace, giving travelers the opportunity to savor the journey and interact with fellow passengers.
- **Bicycle Tours**: Explore destinations by bicycle and immerse yourself in the local scenery and culture at a leisurely pace. Bicycle tours offer the freedom to explore off-the-beaten-path routes, scenic countryside, and charming villages inaccessible by car. Pedal through vineyards, along coastal roads, or through historic towns, stopping to interact with locals, sample regional cuisine, and appreciate the beauty of the surroundings.
- **Walking Holidays**: Embark on walking holidays or trekking adventures that allow you to explore destinations on foot. Whether it's hiking through national parks, walking along ancient pilgrimage routes, or strolling through historic city centers, walking holidays provide an intimate and immersive way to experience a destination. Take time to appreciate the

sights, sounds, and sensations of the journey while connecting with nature and local communities along the way.

- **River Cruises**: Discover destinations from a different perspective on a river cruise, navigating scenic waterways and exploring charming towns and cities along the route. River cruises offer a relaxed and intimate travel experience, with smaller vessels providing opportunities for deeper exploration and interaction with local culture. Enjoy onboard amenities, guided excursions, and shore visits that showcase the unique heritage and attractions of each destination.

- **Deep-Sea Fishing**: At many ocean cities, there are opportunities to charter a boat for a day of deep-sea fishing. This can be an exhilarating adventure for fishing enthusiasts seeking to catch large game fish in open waters. Plus, you have an entire day to gaze out at the ocean. As a kid, our family went deep sea fishing on the Atlantic side of Florida, and my sister caught the prize sailfish for the season for that port. It took quite a while to reel it in and made it an extremely exciting day.

- **Homestays and Farm Stays**: Immerse yourself in local life by staying with host families, participating in farm stays, or booking accommodations in guesthouses and bed-and-breakfasts run by local residents. Homestays and farm stays offer authentic cultural experiences that allow travelers to learn about traditional customs, cuisine, and daily life from their hosts. Engage in activities such as cooking classes, farm work, or cultural exchanges to deepen your connection with the local community.

- **Volunteer Travel**: Combine travel with meaningful volunteer work by participating in volunteer programs and community projects around the world. Volunteer travel opportunities range from environmental conservation projects and wildlife rehabilitation to teaching English, assisting with sustainable development initiatives, and supporting local NGOs. Volunteering allows travelers to make a positive impact while gaining insights into local challenges and contributing to community development.

- **Cultural Immersion Programs**: Enroll in cultural immersion programs, language courses, or workshops that offer opportunities to learn firsthand about local traditions, arts, and crafts. Participate in cooking classes, traditional music and dance workshops, handicraft demonstrations, or spiritual retreats led by local experts. Engage with artisans, performers, and community leaders to gain a deeper understanding of cultural heritage and traditions.
- **Slow Boat Journeys**: Travel by slow boat or traditional watercraft along rivers, canals, or coastlines, and experience the tranquility and rhythm of life on the water. Slow boat journeys provide a unique perspective on destinations and allow travelers to observe daily life along riverbanks, visit remote villages, and witness traditional fishing techniques. Slow boat travel encourages relaxation, reflection, and connection with the natural environment.
- **Self-Drive Adventures**: Explore destinations at your own pace on self-drive adventures. Rent a car or camper van to journey along scenic routes and explore off-the-beaten-path destinations. Self-drive adventures offer flexibility and freedom to stop whenever and wherever you choose and allow for spontaneous discoveries and scenic detours along the way. Take time to explore local markets, picnic in scenic spots, and to interact with locals at roadside cafes and attractions.
- **Culinary Tours and Food Experiences**: Discover the flavors and culinary traditions of a destination through culinary tours, food tastings, and cooking classes. Explore local markets, sample street food, and dine at traditional eateries to savor authentic cuisine and regional specialties. Engage with local chefs, food artisans, and producers to learn about ingredients, cooking techniques, and cultural influences that shape the local gastronomy.

By embracing slow travel options, travelers can cultivate meaningful connections, deepen their understanding of local culture, and create memorable experiences beyond traditional tourism. Whether exploring by train, bicycle, boat, or on foot, slow travel allows for greater immersion, appreciation, and enjoyment of the journey and destination alike.

Off-the-Beaten-Path Adventures

Off-the-beaten-path adventures can take travelers to a wide range of destinations around the world, from remote wilderness areas to hidden gems in bustling cities. Here are some ideas of where to go for off-the-beaten-path adventures:

- **National Parks and Protected Areas**: Explore lesser-known national parks, nature reserves, and wilderness areas that offer opportunities for hiking, wildlife watching, and outdoor adventures. Consider destinations such as Wrangell-St. Elias National Park in Alaska, Namib-Naukluft National Park in Namibia, or Retezat National Park in Romania for off-the-beaten-path experiences in stunning natural landscapes.
- **Island Getaways**: Discover secluded islands and remote archipelagos that offer tranquil beaches, crystal-clear waters, and pristine marine environments. Consider destinations such as the Azores in Portugal, the Outer Hebrides in Scotland, or the Andaman Islands in India for off-the-beaten-path island escape away from the tourist crowds.
- **Rural Villages and Countryside**: Explore rural villages, farming communities, and countryside regions that offer a glimpse into traditional ways of life and cultural heritage. Consider destinations such as the Cotswolds in England, the Mekong Delta in Vietnam, or the Atlas Mountains in Morocco for off-the-beaten-path experiences in scenic rural settings.
- **Historic Towns and Ancient Sites**: Discover historic towns, ancient ruins, and archaeological sites that are less visited by tourists but offer rich cultural and historical significance. Consider destinations such as Matera in Italy, Hampi in India, or Tikal in Guatemala for off-the-beaten-path experiences immersed in history and heritage.
- **Offshore and Remote Islands**: Explore offshore and remote islands that offer unique ecosystems, wildlife habitats, and cultural experiences. Consider destinations such as the Faroe

Islands, Easter Island, or the Solomon Islands for off-the-beaten-path island adventures that promise solitude, serenity, and natural beauty.

- **Road Trip Routes**: Embark on road trips along scenic routes and backroads that offer opportunities for exploration and discovery off the beaten path. Consider driving the North Coast 500 in Scotland, the Ring Road in Iceland, or the Karakoram Highway in Pakistan for off-the-beaten-path adventures with breathtaking landscapes and hidden gems along the way.
- **Mountain and Highland Regions**: Explore mountainous and highland regions that offer rugged terrain, alpine landscapes, and remote villages. Consider destinations such as the Caucasus Mountains in Georgia, the Dolomites in Italy, or the Pamir Mountains in Tajikistan for off-the-beaten-path experiences in dramatic mountain scenery.
- **Desert Landscapes**: Discover remote deserts and arid landscapes that offer solitude, serenity, and stunning natural beauty. Consider destinations such as the Atacama Desert in Chile, the Sahara Desert in Morocco, or the Gobi Desert in Mongolia for off-the-beaten-path adventures in vast and otherworldly environments.

When planning off-the-beaten-path adventures, it's essential to research and prepare accordingly as these destinations may have limited infrastructure, services, and amenities compared to more popular tourist destinations. Additionally, travelers should respect local customs, traditions, and environmental conservation efforts to ensure a positive and sustainable experience for both themselves and the communities they visit.

Cultural Immersion Travel

Cultural immersion travel allows travelers to deeply engage with local communities, traditions, and ways of life, fostering meaningful connections and enriching experiences. Here are some destinations where travelers can go for cultural immersion travel:

- **Historic Cities**: Explore historic cities with rich cultural heritage, architectural landmarks, and vibrant street life. Consider destinations such as Kyoto in Japan, Florence in Italy, or Istanbul in Turkey for cultural experiences immersed in art, history, and tradition.
- **Indigenous Communities**: Visit indigenous communities and tribal villages to learn about traditional customs, rituals, and lifestyles. Consider destinations such as the Maasai Mara in Kenya, the Navajo Nation in the United States, or the Māori villages in New Zealand for cultural immersion experiences with indigenous people.
- **Rural Villages**: Stay in rural villages and farming communities to experience authentic rural life and agricultural traditions. Consider destinations such as Tuscany in Italy, Ubud in Bali, or the Mekong Delta in Vietnam for cultural immersion experiences in picturesque countryside settings.
- **Ethnic Enclaves**: Explore ethnic enclaves and cultural neighborhoods within cities that offer a diverse array of cuisines, languages, and traditions. Consider destinations such as Chinatown in San Francisco, Little India in Singapore, or the Medina in Marrakech for cultural immersion experiences within multicultural urban environments.
- **Religious Pilgrimage Sites**: Visit religious pilgrimage sites and sacred destinations to participate in spiritual rituals, festivals, and ceremonies. Consider destinations such as Varanasi in India, Lourdes in France, or Santiago de Compostela in Spain for cultural immersion experiences centered around religious and spiritual traditions.
- **Artisan Workshops**: Visit artisan workshops and craft villages to learn about traditional craftsmanship and artisanal techniques. Consider destinations such as Oaxaca in Mexico for pottery and weaving, Fez in Morocco for leatherwork and metalwork, or Ubrique in Spain for leather goods and handbags for cultural immersion experiences immersed in artisanal traditions.
- **Cultural Festivals**: Attend cultural festivals and celebrations that showcase local music, dance, food, and traditions.

Consider destinations such as Rio de Janeiro in Brazil for Carnival, Jaipur in India for Diwali, or Munich in Germany for Oktoberfest for cultural immersion experiences during festive occasions.

- **Homestays and Community-Based Tourism**: Stay with local families or participate in community-based tourism initiatives to experience daily life and traditions firsthand. Consider destinations such as homestays in rural villages in Nepal, community-based ecotourism projects in Costa Rica, or cultural exchange programs in Japan for cultural immersion experiences with local communities.
- **Language Immersion Programs**: Participate in language immersion programs or language schools to learn a new language and immerse yourself in the local culture. Consider destinations such as Barcelona in Spain for Spanish immersion, Paris in France for French immersion, or Tokyo in Japan for Japanese immersion for cultural immersion experiences combined with language learning.
- **Cultural Heritage Sites**: Explore UNESCO World Heritage Sites and cultural heritage sites that preserve and showcase important aspects of human history and civilization. Consider destinations such as Angkor Wat in Cambodia, Petra in Jordan, or Machu Picchu in Peru for cultural immersion experiences immersed in ancient civilizations and architectural wonders.

When planning cultural immersion travel, it's essential to approach the experience with an open mind, respect for local customs and traditions, and a willingness to engage with the local community in a meaningful and respectful manner. By immersing yourself in the culture of a destination, you can gain a deeper understanding of its people, traditions, and way of life, creating lasting memories and meaningful connections along the way.

Multigenerational Travel

Multigenerational travel involves planning trips that cater to the needs and interests of travelers of different ages, from children to grandparents. Here are some destinations suitable for multigenerational travel:

- **Family-Friendly Resorts**: Choose family-friendly resorts and all-inclusive hotels that offer a wide range of amenities and activities for travelers of all ages. Many family resorts feature kids' clubs, swimming pools, water parks, sports facilities, and entertainment options to keep everyone entertained and engaged.
- **Theme Parks**: Visit theme parks and amusement parks that offer attractions and entertainment suitable for all ages. Destinations such as Disneyland Resort in California, Walt Disney World Resort in Florida, or Universal Studios in Florida provide rides, shows, and experiences that appeal to children, teenagers, and adults alike.
- **Beach Destinations**: Opt for beach destinations with calm waters, sandy shores, and family-friendly activities, such as swimming, snorkeling, sandcastle building, and beach volleyball. Destinations such as Maui in Hawaii, Cancun in Mexico, or the Outer Banks in North Carolina offer a variety of beachfront accommodations and water-based activities for multigenerational travelers.
- **National Parks**: Explore national parks and natural attractions that offer opportunities for outdoor adventure and exploration. Many national parks provide hiking trails, scenic viewpoints, wildlife viewing, and educational programs suitable for families with children and grandparents. Consider destinations such as Yellowstone National Park, Grand Canyon National Park, or Acadia National Park for multigenerational outdoor adventures.
- **Cultural Cities**: Visit cultural cities and historic destinations that offer a blend of educational experiences, sightseeing, and cultural immersion. Cities such as London, Paris, Rome, or Kyoto provide opportunities to explore museums, historic landmarks, and cultural attractions that appeal to travelers of all ages.

- **Cruise Vacations:** Consider booking a multigenerational cruise vacation that offers a variety of onboard activities, dining options, and shore excursions for travelers of different ages. Many cruise lines provide family-friendly amenities such as children's clubs, teen lounges, live entertainment, and multigenerational dining experiences.
- **Rural Retreats**: Escape to rural retreats and countryside destinations that offer peace, tranquility, and opportunities for outdoor recreation. Rent a vacation home or farmhouse in scenic rural settings where families can enjoy activities such as hiking, biking, fishing, or simply relaxing and reconnecting with nature.
- **Adventure Tours**: Embark on adventure tours and guided expeditions that offer thrilling experiences suitable for multigenerational travelers. Consider destinations such as Costa Rica for zip-lining and wildlife tours, Alaska for whale watching and glacier cruises, or Iceland for volcano hikes and hot spring baths.
- **Cultural Immersion Trips**: Plan cultural immersion trips that allow multigenerational travelers to learn about different cultures, traditions, and ways of life. Consider destinations such as Japan for tea ceremonies and samurai experiences, Morocco for camel treks and desert camping, or India for temple visits and spice market tours.
- **Family Reunions**: Organize family reunions and gatherings in destinations that offer accommodations, facilities, and activities suitable for large groups of multigenerational travelers. Rent a vacation home, villa, or resort property where families can come together to celebrate milestones, share meals, and create cherished memories.

When planning multigenerational travel, it's essential to consider the interests, preferences, and needs of travelers of different ages as well as to choose destinations and activities that offer something for everyone. By selecting destinations that cater to multigenerational travelers, families can create memorable experiences and strengthen bonds across generations.

Adventure Travel

Adventure travel appeals to those seeking thrilling experiences and adrenaline-pumping activities in diverse and often rugged landscapes. Here are some destinations renowned for adventure travel:

- **Nepal**: Known for its towering Himalayan peaks, Nepal offers unparalleled opportunities for trekking, mountaineering, and adventure sports. Travelers can embark on the legendary Everest Base Camp trek, summit peaks like Annapurna or Langtang, or experience the thrills of whitewater rafting, paragliding, and bungee jumping.
- **New Zealand**: With its stunning landscapes and wide range of outdoor activities, New Zealand is a haven for adventure travelers. Explore the rugged beauty of Fiordland National Park, go hiking in the Southern Alps, try bungee jumping in Queenstown, or experience the thrill of jet boating and skydiving.
- **Costa Rica**: Costa Rica is a paradise for eco-adventurers and offers lush rainforests, active volcanoes, and pristine beaches. Travelers can zip-line through the canopy, hike to remote waterfalls, go whitewater rafting on jungle rivers, or explore the rich biodiversity of national parks like Manuel Antonio and Corcovado.
- **Peru**: Home to the iconic Machu Picchu, Peru offers a wealth of adventure opportunities, from trekking the Inca Trail to exploring the Amazon rainforest. Travelers can hike the Colca Canyon, go sandboarding in the desert oasis of Huacachina, or navigate the whitewater rapids of the Urubamba River.
- **Iceland**: With its dramatic landscapes of glaciers, volcanoes, and geothermal wonders, Iceland is a playground for outdoor enthusiasts. Adventure travelers can go glacier hiking, ice climbing, and snowmobiling on glaciers, explore lava caves, or soak in natural hot springs under the Northern Lights.
- **Patagonia**: Straddling the southernmost regions of Chile and Argentina, Patagonia offers some of the world's most remote and breathtaking wilderness areas. Travelers can trek in Torres del Paine National Park, go kayaking among glaciers in Tierra

del Fuego, or embark on multi-day expeditions in the rugged Andes.

- **Alaska**: Known for its vast wilderness and rugged terrain, Alaska offers a wide range of adventure activities, from bear viewing and whale watching to glacier hiking and dog sledding. Travelers can explore Denali National Park, paddle through fjords in Kenai Fjords National Park, or go ice climbing on towering glaciers.
- **Bhutan**: Tucked away in the eastern Himalayas, Bhutan offers a unique blend of cultural immersion and outdoor adventure. Travelers can trek the challenging Snowman Trek, go mountain biking through pristine landscapes, or experience the ancient tradition of archery in remote villages.
- **South Africa**: South Africa is a diverse and thrilling destination for adventure travelers and offers opportunities for safaris, shark cage diving, and wilderness hikes. Travelers can explore Kruger National Park, go bungee jumping at Bloukrans Bridge, or hike to the top of Table Mountain for panoramic views of Cape Town.
- **Australia**: From the rugged Outback to the pristine coastlines, Australia offers endless adventure possibilities. Travelers can dive the Great Barrier Reef, hike in the ancient landscapes of the Red Centre, go surfing on world-class waves, or explore the remote wilderness of Tasmania.

These destinations are just a starting point for adventure travelers who seek the thrill of exploration and the challenge of pushing their limits in some of the world's most spectacular and untamed landscapes. Whether trekking to remote mountain summits, exploring dense rainforests, or diving into crystal-clear waters, adventure travel offers unforgettable experiences for those who dare to venture off the beaten path.

Culinary Experiences Travel

Culinary experiences travel, also known as food tourism or gastronomic tourism, involves exploring destinations known for their culinary traditions, local cuisine, and food culture. Here are some places renowned for culinary experiences travel:

- **Italy**: Renowned for its delicious cuisine, Italy offers a wealth of culinary experiences for food lovers. Travelers can indulge in authentic pasta dishes, wood-fired pizzas, and creamy gelato, as well as regional specialties such as risotto in Lombardy, fresh seafood in Sicily, and truffles in Piedmont.
- **France**: With its rich culinary heritage and Michelin-starred restaurants, France is a paradise for food enthusiasts. Travelers can savor gourmet delights such as foie gras in the Dordogne, coq au vin in Burgundy, and croissants in Paris, as well as regional wines and cheeses in the Loire Valley and Bordeaux.
- **Japan**: Known for its precision and attention to detail, Japanese cuisine offers a diverse array of flavors and textures. Travelers can sample sushi and sashimi in Tokyo, ramen in Fukuoka, and tempura in Kyoto, as well as regional specialties such as okonomiyaki in Hiroshima and takoyaki in Osaka.
- **Spain**: Spain is celebrated for its vibrant food culture and tapas tradition. Travelers can feast on paella in Valencia, pintxos in San Sebastian, and gazpacho in Andalusia as well as regional delicacies such as jamón ibérico in Extremadura and seafood in Galicia.
- **Thailand**: With its bold flavors and aromatic spices, Thai cuisine offers a tantalizing culinary journey. Travelers can sample street food in Bangkok, pad thai in Chiang Mai, and green curry in Phuket as well as regional dishes such as som tam in Isaan and khao soi in Northern Thailand.
- **Mexico**: Mexico's vibrant food scene boasts a rich tapestry of flavors, colors, and textures. Travelers can enjoy tacos al pastor in Mexico City, ceviche in Baja California, and mole poblano in Oaxaca as well as street food specialties such as elote and tamales.
- **India**: With its diverse regional cuisines, India offers a feast for the senses. Travelers can savor curries in Delhi, dosas in Chennai, and biryani in Hyderabad as well as street food delights such as chaat in Mumbai and vada pav in Pune.

- **Vietnam**: Vietnamese cuisine is renowned for its fresh ingredients and complex flavors. Travelers can sample pho in Hanoi, banh mi in Ho Chi Minh City, and fresh seafood in coastal towns like Da Nang and Nha Trang.
- **Greece**: Greece's Mediterranean cuisine is celebrated for its simplicity and freshness. Travelers can enjoy moussaka in Athens, souvlaki in Santorini, and fresh seafood on the islands of Crete and Mykonos.
- **Morocco**: Moroccan cuisine offers a tantalizing blend of spices, flavors, and textures. Travelers can savor tagine in Marrakech, couscous in Fes, and pastilla in Casablanca, as well as street food specialties such as harira and msemen.

These destinations offer a wealth of culinary experiences, from fine dining at Michelin-starred restaurants to sampling street food at bustling markets and food stalls. Culinary experiences travel allows travelers to immerse themselves in the local food culture, learn about traditional cooking techniques, and savor the unique flavors and ingredients of each destination.

Cruise Travel

Cruise travel offers a convenient and enjoyable way to explore multiple destinations while enjoying luxurious amenities and entertainment onboard. Here are some popular destinations for cruise travel:

- **Caribbean**: Cruise ships ply the crystal-clear waters of the Caribbean, stopping at idyllic islands with pristine beaches, lush rainforests, and vibrant cultures. Itineraries often include stops at destinations such as the Bahamas, Jamaica, the Cayman Islands, and St. Maarten and offer opportunities for snorkeling, beachcombing, and exploring historic towns.
- **Mediterranean**: Cruising the Mediterranean allows travelers to visit iconic cities, ancient ruins, and picturesque coastal villages. Itineraries typically include ports of call in Italy (such as Venice, Rome, and Naples), Greece (including Athens, Santorini, and Mykonos), Spain (such as Barcelona and Palma de Mallorca), and France (including Marseille and Nice).

- **Alaska**: Cruising through Alaska's Inside Passage offers breathtaking views of glaciers, fjords, and wildlife-rich wilderness areas. Itineraries often include stops at ports such as Juneau, Skagway, and Ketchikan as well as scenic cruising through Glacier Bay or Tracy Arm Fjord, allowing passengers to spot whales, eagles, and bears.
- **Norwegian Fjords**: Cruising through Norway's fjords is a scenic and unforgettable experience with towering cliffs, cascading waterfalls, and charming coastal villages. Itineraries typically include ports such as Bergen, Geiranger, and Flam as well as scenic cruising through the stunning landscapes of Sognefjord and Hardangerfjord.
- **South Pacific**: Cruising the South Pacific allows travelers to visit tropical paradises with palm-fringed beaches, turquoise lagoons, and vibrant coral reefs. Itineraries often include stops at destinations such as Tahiti, Bora Bora, Fiji, and the Cook Islands and offer opportunities for snorkeling, diving, and cultural experiences.
- **Northern Europe**: Cruising in Northern Europe offers a chance to explore historic cities, medieval castles, and scenic landscapes. Itineraries typically include ports such as Copenhagen, Stockholm, St. Petersburg, and Tallinn as well as scenic cruising through the Norwegian coastline and the Baltic Sea.
- **Hawaii**: Cruising around the Hawaiian Islands allows travelers to experience the Aloha spirit while visiting beautiful beaches, volcanic landscapes, and cultural sites. Itineraries often include stops at ports such as Honolulu, Maui, Kauai, and the Big Island and offer opportunities for snorkeling, surfing, and exploring lava fields.
- **Australia and New Zealand**: Cruising in Australia and New Zealand offers a chance to explore diverse landscapes, from rugged coastlines and lush rainforests to vibrant cities and Maori culture. Itineraries typically include ports such as Sydney, Auckland, Melbourne, and Wellington as well as scenic cruising through the Milford Sound and the Great Barrier Reef.

- **Transatlantic**: Transatlantic cruises offer a leisurely journey across the Atlantic Ocean, often with stops at ports in Europe and North America. Itineraries may include ports such as Southampton, New York City, Lisbon, and Barcelona, which allows passengers to explore historic landmarks, cultural attractions, and culinary delights along the way.
- **Antarctica**: Expedition cruises to Antarctica offer a once-in-a-lifetime opportunity to explore the world's southernmost continent with its pristine wilderness, icebergs, and diverse wildlife. Itineraries typically depart from ports in Argentina or Chile and include stops at the Antarctic Peninsula, South Shetland Islands, and Falkland Islands, allowing passengers to witness penguins, seals, and whales in their natural habitat.

These destinations offer a variety of experiences for cruise travelers, from scenic cruising and wildlife viewing to cultural immersion and outdoor adventures. Whether exploring tropical islands, historic cities, or remote wilderness areas, cruise travel provides a convenient and enjoyable way to see the world.

Road Trips

Road trips offer the freedom to explore diverse landscapes, charming towns, and hidden gems along scenic routes. Here are some popular destinations for road trips:

- **Pacific Coast Highway (California, USA)**: Also known as Highway 1, this iconic route stretches along the California coastline and offers breathtaking ocean views, dramatic cliffs, and picturesque seaside towns such as Big Sur, Monterey, and Santa Barbara.
- **Great Ocean Road (Victoria, Australia)**: This stunning coastal drive winds along the rugged southern coast of Victoria and showcases dramatic rock formations, pristine beaches, and lush rainforests. Highlights include the Twelve Apostles, Loch Ard Gorge, and the seaside town of Lorne.
- **Ring Road (Iceland)**: Iceland's Ring Road circumnavigates the entire island and passes by otherworldly landscapes such as

glaciers, waterfalls, volcanic craters, and geothermal hot springs. Highlights include the Golden Circle, Jökulsárlón Glacier Lagoon, and the volcanic landscapes of the Westfjords.

- **Route 66 (USA)**: Known as the "Mother Road," Route 66 is a historic highway that stretches from Chicago to Los Angeles and passes by iconic American landmarks, quirky roadside attractions, and through charming small towns. Highlights include the Grand Canyon, Cadillac Ranch, and the Santa Monica Pier.

- **The Garden Route (South Africa)**: The Garden Route winds along the coast of South Africa's Western Cape and offers stunning scenery, diverse wildlife, and outdoor adventures. Highlights include the Tsitsikamma National Park, Knysna Lagoon, and the ostrich farms of Oudtshoorn.

- **North Coast 500 (Scotland)**: Scotland's North Coast 500 is a scenic route that loops around the northern Highlands and offers breathtaking views of rugged coastline, historic castles, and remote villages. Highlights include the Isle of Skye, Dunrobin Castle, and the coastal town of Durness.

- **Amalfi Coast (Italy)**: Italy's Amalfi Coast is a picturesque stretch of coastline dotted with colorful cliffside villages, lemon groves, and terraced vineyards. The winding coastal road offers stunning views of the Mediterranean Sea with highlights that include Positano, Amalfi, and Ravello.

- **Trollstigen (Norway)**: Trollstigen, or the Troll's Path, is a scenic mountain road that winds through the Norwegian fjords and offers breathtaking views of waterfalls, snow-capped peaks, and lush valleys. Highlights include the Trollstigen viewpoint, Geirangerfjord, and the village of Åndalsnes.

- **Cabot Trail (Nova Scotia, Canada)**: The Cabot Trail is a scenic drive that loops around the northern tip of Nova Scotia's Cape Breton Island and offers stunning views of rugged coastline, highland plateaus, and quaint fishing villages. Highlights include Cape Breton Highlands National Park, the Skyline Trail, and the village of Baddeck.

- **Wild Atlantic Way (Ireland)**: Ireland's Wild Atlantic Way is one of the world's longest coastal routes, stretching along the rugged western coastline from Donegal to Cork. Highlights include the Cliffs of Moher, the Ring of Kerry, and the Dingle Peninsula.

- These road trip destinations offer a variety of landscapes, attractions, and experiences for travelers seeking adventure, scenic beauty, and cultural immersion on the open road. Whether cruising along coastal highways, winding through mountain passes, or exploring remote wilderness areas, road trips provide an unforgettable journey of discovery and exploration.

Cultural Heritage Tours

Cultural heritage tours offer travelers the opportunity to explore historical sites, ancient ruins, museums, and monuments that showcase a destination's rich cultural heritage and history. Here are some popular destinations for cultural heritage tours:

- **Egypt**: Egypt is home to some of the world's most iconic cultural heritage sites, including the Pyramids of Giza, the Sphinx, and the temples of Luxor and Karnak. Travelers can also explore the Valley of the Kings, the Egyptian Museum in Cairo, and the ancient city of Alexandria.
- **Italy**: Italy is a treasure trove of cultural heritage with historic cities, ancient ruins, and Renaissance art and architecture. Highlights include the Colosseum and Roman Forum in Rome, the Uffizi Gallery and Duomo in Florence, and the canals of Venice.
- **Greece**: Greece boasts a rich cultural heritage dating back thousands of years and has iconic landmarks such as the Acropolis and Parthenon in Athens, the ancient city of Delphi, and the archaeological site of Knossos on the island of Crete.
- **Peru**: Peru is home to the ancient Inca civilization and has cultural heritage sites such as Machu Picchu, the Sacred Valley, and the city of Cusco. Travelers can also explore the Nazca Lines, the Colca Canyon, and the colonial architecture of Lima.

- **China**: China's cultural heritage spans thousands of years and has landmarks such as the Great Wall, the Forbidden City, and the Terracotta Army. Travelers can also visit ancient temples and gardens in cities like Beijing, Xi'an, and Suzhou.
- **India**: India is a land of diverse cultural heritage with historic cities, temples, and palaces dating back centuries. Highlights include the Taj Mahal in Agra, the temples of Khajuraho, and the forts and palaces of Rajasthan.
- **Turkey**: Turkey is a crossroads of cultures with a rich heritage that includes ancient ruins, Byzantine churches, and Ottoman architecture. Highlights include the Hagia Sophia and Blue Mosque in Istanbul, the ruins of Ephesus, and the fairy chimneys of Cappadocia.
- **Mexico**: Mexico's cultural heritage is a blend of indigenous and colonial influences with landmarks such as the ancient city of Teotihuacan, the Mayan ruins of Chichen Itza, and the colonial architecture of Mexico City and Oaxaca.
- **Cambodia**: Cambodia is home to the ancient temple complex of Angkor Wat as well as other cultural heritage sites such as the Royal Palace in Phnom Penh and the floating villages of Tonle Sap Lake.
- **Jordan**: Jordan boasts a rich cultural heritage and has landmarks such as the ancient city of Petra, the Roman ruins of Jerash, and the desert landscapes of Wadi Rum. Travelers can also visit the Dead Sea, Mount Nebo, and the crusader castles of Ajloun and Kerak.

These destinations offer a wealth of cultural heritage sites and experiences for travelers interested in exploring the history, art, and architecture of different civilizations and time periods. Whether visiting ancient ruins, admiring religious monuments, or exploring historic cities, cultural heritage tours provide a deeper understanding of the world's diverse cultural heritage and the people who shaped it.

Chapter 9

Side Jobs

"To find joy in work is to discover the fountain of youth."

—Pearl S. Buck

Okay, maybe the thing that would truly make you happy is to start a little side business. The next question is, what kind of business? Well, for goodness sakes, don't limit yourself. Read through the ideas in this chapter and see if something jumps out at you. If you have an idea of what you want, you ought to at least see if there is something here you have never even thought of. I can almost guarantee you haven't thought of some of these, and you might want to try one of these instead. Some of these require a certain skill, some you may have to learn as you go, and others may require training. Some of these just require a fun attitude. But I will start first with some of the more common suggestions.

Some Typical Suggestions

These side business ideas offer opportunities to leverage your skills, interests, and passions into profitable ventures. Whether you're pursuing a creative hobby, sharing your expertise, or providing valuable services to others, these can be both rewarding and fulfilling.

- **Consulting**: Leverage your expertise and experience by offering consulting services in your field of knowledge. Provide advice, guidance, and solutions to businesses or individuals seeking your expertise.
- **Online Tutoring**: Share your knowledge and skills by offering online tutoring services in subjects you're proficient in. Tutor students of all ages in academic subjects, language learning, or specialized skills such as music or coding.
- **Freelance Writing**: Start a freelance writing business, and offer your writing services to businesses, publications, or websites.

Offer copywriting, ghostwriting, and marketing material content (such as writing articles, blogs, social posts, product descriptions, instruction manuals, and books) to clients in various industries.

- **Handmade Crafts**: Turn your creative talents into a profitable business by selling handmade crafts online or at local markets and craft fairs. Create and sell items such as jewelry, pottery, candles, or knitted goods.
- **E-commerce Store**: Start an e-commerce store selling products in a niche market you're passionate about. Source or create unique products such as handmade goods, vintage items, or specialty products to sell online.
- **Pet Sitting or Dog Walking**: Offer pet sitting or dog walking services to pet owners in your community. Care for pets while their owners are away and provide companionship, exercise, and basic care services.
- **Home Staging**: Use your creativity and design skills to start a home staging business. Help homeowners prepare their properties for sale by decluttering, organizing, and styling spaces to attract potential buyers.
- **Personal Chef Services**: Offer personal chef services to busy individuals or families who don't have time to cook. Prepare customized meals in clients' homes based on their dietary preferences and nutritional needs.
- **Photography Services**: Start a photography business offering services such as portrait photography, event photography, or real estate photography. Capture special moments and memories for clients while showcasing your artistic vision.
- **Social Media Management**: Help businesses improve their online presence by offering social media management services. Manage clients' social media accounts, create content, engage with followers, and analyze performance metrics.
- **Virtual Assistant**: Provide virtual assistant services to busy professionals or entrepreneurs who need help with administrative tasks, email management, scheduling, or research.

- **Fitness Coaching**: Use your passion for health and fitness to become a fitness coach or personal trainer. Offer one-on-one coaching sessions, group fitness classes, or online fitness programs to help clients achieve their wellness goals.
- **Tour Guide**: Share your knowledge and passion for your city or region by becoming a tour guide. Lead walking tours, historical tours, or specialized tours focusing on food, art, or culture for tourists and visitors.
- **Home Renovation Services**: Use your handyman skills to offer home renovation or repair services to homeowners. Help clients with small renovation projects, repairs, or upgrades to improve their homes' functionality and aesthetics.
- **Language Translation**: Offer language translation services to businesses or individuals who need documents, websites, or marketing materials translated into different languages.
- **Gardening Services**: Provide gardening services to homeowners who need help maintaining their gardens and outdoor spaces. Offer services such as lawn care, landscaping, planting, or garden maintenance.
- **Financial Planning**: Use your knowledge of finance and investments to offer financial planning services to individuals or families. Help clients create personalized financial plans, manage investments, and achieve their financial goals.
- **Home Organizing**: Start a home organizing business helping clients declutter, organize, and optimize their living spaces. Offer services such as closet organization, kitchen organization, or home office organization.
- **Car Detailing**: Start a car detailing business offering professional cleaning and detailing services to car owners. Clean, polish, and restore vehicles' interiors and exteriors to make them look brand new.
- **Life Coaching**: Become a certified life coach and offer coaching services to clients seeking guidance and support in achieving personal or professional goals. Help clients overcome challenges, gain clarity, and create fulfilling lives.

Unusual Ideas

Here are some unusual side business ideas. These offer opportunities to explore niche markets, leverage unique skills and interests, and create innovative and memorable experiences for customers. Whether you're passionate about sustainability, creativity, or adventure, these can be both fulfilling and profitable.

- **Beekeeping Products**: Start a business selling honey, beeswax candles, and other bee-related products. Harvest honey from your own beehives or source from local beekeepers to create unique and natural products.
- **Escape Room Design**: Design and build custom escape rooms for events, parties, or businesses. Create immersive and challenging puzzles, themes, and scenarios for players to solve and escape from.
- **Mystery Dinner Parties**: Host mystery dinner parties where guests solve a fictional murder mystery while enjoying a gourmet meal. Provide scripts, costumes, and clues to create an interactive and entertaining experience.
- **Tiny House Construction**: Build and sell custom tiny houses for individuals seeking minimalist and eco-friendly living solutions. Offer customizable designs, sustainable materials, and compact living options.
- **Vintage Trailer Rentals**: Start a business renting out vintage trailers for camping trips, festivals, or special events. Restore and refurbish vintage trailers to create unique and nostalgic accommodations for travelers.
- **Mobile Pet Grooming**: Offer mobile pet grooming services where you visit clients' homes to groom their pets in a convenient and stress-free environment. Provide services such as bathing, grooming, and nail trimming for dogs and cats.
- **Sustainable Fashion**: Start a business selling eco-friendly and sustainable fashion products such as upcycled clothing, organic fabrics, or fair-trade accessories. Promote ethical and environmentally conscious fashion choices to consumers.
- **Aquaponics Farming**: Set up an aquaponics farm to grow organic vegetables and raise fish in a sustainable and

symbiotic system. Sell fresh produce and fish to local markets, restaurants, or community-supported agriculture programs.

- **Virtual Reality Arcade**: Create a virtual reality arcade where customers can experience immersive VR games, simulations, and experiences. Offer VR equipment rentals, gaming sessions, and VR-themed events for parties and corporate events.
- **Mobile Bicycle Repair**: Offer mobile bicycle repair services where you visit clients' homes or workplaces to perform bike repairs, maintenance, and tune-ups. Provide convenient and personalized service for cyclists in your community.
- **Indoor Vertical Farming**: Start an indoor vertical farming business using hydroponic or aeroponic systems to grow crops vertically in controlled environments. Produce fresh herbs, vegetables, and microgreens year-round for local markets and restaurants.
- **Custom Pinata Design**: Create custom pinatas for parties, events, and celebrations. Design and craft unique pinatas in various shapes, themes, and sizes to suit customers' preferences and occasions.
- **Virtual Pet Training**: Offer virtual pet training sessions and consultations to pet owners using video conferencing platforms. Provide personalized training plans, behavior modification techniques, and expert advice for pet owners seeking guidance.
- **Sustainable Living Workshops**: Host workshops and classes on sustainable living practices such as composting, zero waste living, and renewable energy. Educate and empower individuals to adopt eco-friendly habits and reduce their environmental footprint.
- **Custom Skateboard Design**: Design and create custom skateboards, longboards, and cruisers for skateboard enthusiasts. Offer customizable designs, graphics, and finishes to create personalized and one-of-a-kind skateboards.
- **Exotic Plant Nursery**: Start a nursery specializing in rare and exotic plants, succulents, and tropical foliage. Source unique

plant varieties from around the world, and sell them to collectors, enthusiasts, and landscaping professionals.

- **Alpaca Farm Tours**: Offer guided tours of an alpaca farm where visitors can learn about alpacas, their care, and fiber production. Provide hands-on experiences such as feeding, grooming, and interacting with the alpacas.
- **Vintage Arcade Restoration**: Restore and refurbish vintage arcade games and pinball machines for collectors and enthusiasts. Bring classic arcade games back to life by repairing and restoring them to their original condition.
- **Urbex Photography Tours**: Lead photography tours focused on urban exploration (urbex), where participants can discover and photograph abandoned buildings, industrial sites, and urban decay. Provide guidance on photography techniques and safety protocols for exploring abandoned spaces.
- **Customized Sneaker Design**: Customize and personalize sneakers for customers looking for unique and stylish footwear. Offer custom paint jobs, designs, and modifications to transform ordinary sneakers into wearable works of art.

Very Unconventional

Here we get close to, and sometimes cross into, the bizarre. These side business ideas offer opportunities to tap into niche markets, provide unique experiences, and explore unconventional interests. Whether you're drawn to the mysterious, the unusual, or the downright bizarre, these can be both entertaining and lucrative.

- **Rent-a-Chicken**: Start a business where customers can rent chickens for a temporary period to experience backyard chicken farming without the long-term commitment. Provide everything needed for chicken care, including feed and coop setup.
- **Professional Cuddling Service**: Offer a professional cuddling service where clients can book cuddle sessions with trained cuddle partners for relaxation and comfort. Provide a safe and platonic environment for clients to enjoy the benefits of human touch.

- **Bug Eating Experience**: Create an exotic dining experience where customers can sample edible insects and other bizarre delicacies from around the world. Offer tasting menus featuring insects such as crickets, mealworms, and scorpions prepared in various dishes.
- **Customized Pet Clothing**: Design and create custom clothing and accessories for pets, including outfits, costumes, and accessories tailored to each pet's personality and style. Cater to pet owners who love to dress up their furry friends in unique and unusual attire.
- **Professional Whistling Lessons**: Offer professional whistling lessons for individuals interested in mastering the art of whistling. Teach various whistling techniques, styles, and melodies to students of all ages and skill levels.
- **Paranormal Investigation Tours**: Lead paranormal investigation tours where participants can explore allegedly haunted locations and conduct ghost hunts. Provide equipment such as EMF meters and infrared cameras for detecting supernatural activity.
- **Rent-a-Sloth Experience**: Offer a unique experience where customers can rent sloths for a designated period to spend time with these slow-moving and adorable creatures. Provide educational sessions and guided interactions with the sloths.
- **Professional Plant Whisperer**: Provide professional plant whispering services for individuals struggling to care for their houseplants. Communicate with plants to understand their needs, and offer advice on plant care and maintenance.
- **Custom Fortune Cookie Messages**: Create a business offering customized fortune cookie messages for special occasions, events, or promotions. Write personalized fortunes tailored to each customer's preferences and intended recipients.
- **Rent-a-Fish Tank**: Rent out fish tanks for businesses, events, or home staging purposes. Provide fully stocked and maintained fish tanks on a temporary basis, offering a hassle-free way for customers to enjoy the beauty of aquatic life.

- **Personal UFO Sightings Tours**: Lead guided tours to UFO hotspots and alleged extraterrestrial sighting locations that offer participants the chance to experience close encounters with unidentified flying objects. Provide telescopes and night vision equipment for skywatching.
- **Professional Apology Services**: Offer professional apology services for individuals seeking assistance in crafting sincere and heartfelt apologies. Write apology letters, make apology calls, or conduct apology ceremonies on behalf of clients.
- **Professional Clown Therapy**: Offer clown therapy sessions for individuals seeking laughter, joy, and stress relief. Use clowning techniques, humor, and play to promote emotional well-being and positivity in clients.
- **Custom Bobblehead Sculptures**: Create custom bobblehead sculptures of individuals, pets, or fictional characters based on customer specifications. Offer personalized bobbleheads for gifts, collectibles, or promotional purposes.
- **Lego Sculpture Workshops**: Host Lego sculpture workshops where participants can learn to build elaborate sculptures and creations using Lego bricks. Provide guidance, inspiration, and building tips for aspiring Lego artists.
- **Haunted Doll Adoption Agency**: As mentioned in another chapter, create a business offering haunted doll adoption services, where customers can adopt allegedly haunted dolls with mysterious histories and paranormal activity. Provide adoption certificates and storytelling sessions about each doll's past.
- **Professional Mermaid Performances**: Train as a professional mermaid performer and entertain audiences with underwater performances, swimming routines, and aquatic shows. Embrace the enchantment of mermaid mythology while captivating spectators.

Chapter 10
New Career

"We ought to recognize the profound gulf between the work to which we are 'called' and the work we are forced into as a means of livelihood."

—Dorothy L. Sayers

What if you want more than a side business? Perhaps you want to try something completely new as a career. If that is what will make you happy, then here are some general categories of career opportunities to stay active, engaged, and fulfilled. By exploring new interests, leveraging your skills and experience, and embracing new challenges, you can enjoy a fulfilling and rewarding journey.

- **Consulting**: You can leverage your extensive experience and expertise in your field by offering consulting services. This could involve providing advice, strategic planning, or problem-solving solutions to businesses, organizations, or individuals. You can work independently as a consultant or join a consulting firm specializing in your area of expertise.
- **Freelancing**: Freelancing allows you to work on a flexible schedule and choose projects that align with your skills and interests. You can offer freelance services such as writing, editing, graphic design, web development, consulting, marketing, or virtual assistance. Freelancing platforms like Upwork, Freelancer, and Fiverr provide opportunities to connect with clients and find freelance work.
- **Teaching or Tutoring**: If you have knowledge and expertise in a particular subject area, you can explore opportunities in teaching or tutoring. This could involve teaching courses at community colleges, adult education centers, or online learning platforms. You can also offer private tutoring services to students of all ages, either in person or virtually.

- **Entrepreneurship**: Retirement can be an ideal time for you to pursue entrepreneurial ventures and start your own business. Whether it's launching a small business, opening a boutique store, or starting an online shop, you can turn your hobby, passion, or expertise into a profitable venture. Entrepreneurial opportunities could include e-commerce, a consulting firm, franchise ownership, or a home-based business.

- **Nonprofit Work**: You can work at a nonprofit organization or perform volunteer work as a way to give back to your community and make a positive impact. You can explore opportunities to work for nonprofit organizations in roles such as program management, fundraising, marketing, or administration. Alternatively, you can volunteer your time and skills to support causes you care about, whether it's serving on a board of directors, organizing events, or providing mentorship.

- **Tourism and Hospitality**: If you enjoy travel and hospitality, you can pursue opportunities in the tourism industry. This could involve working as a tour guide, travel agent, hotel concierge, event planner, or cruise ship staff. You can share your knowledge and passion for travel by helping others plan and experience memorable trips and vacations.

- **Health and Wellness**: With a growing emphasis on health and wellness, you can explore opportunities in this field. You can become certified as a personal trainer, yoga instructor, nutrition coach, or wellness consultant. You can work independently, offer group classes, or provide one-on-one coaching to help clients improve their physical and mental well-being.

- **Creative Arts**: Retirement provides the time and freedom for you to explore your creative passions and pursue artistic endeavors. You can pursue a career as a writer, painter, photographer, musician, or craft artisan. You can sell your artwork, exhibit your work at galleries, teach workshops or classes, or offer your creative services for hire.

146

- **Home-Based Businesses**: Perhaps you want to start a home-based business that will allow you to work from the comfort of your own home. This could include opportunities such as freelance services mentioned in the Freelancing section a couple of pages ago, bookkeeping, or e-commerce. Home-based businesses offer flexibility and low overhead costs, making them ideal if you are looking for part-time or supplemental income.
- **Continuing Education**: Retirement provides an opportunity for lifelong learning and personal development. You can explore opportunities for continuing education by taking classes, attending workshops, or pursuing certifications in areas of interest. This could lead to new career opportunities, expand your skill set, or simply provide a sense of fulfillment and enrichment.

Chapter 11
Community Service / Volunteering

"I really believe that volunteerism is the cure for every negative emotion—boredom, loneliness, unhappiness. Busyness takes away the pain. And think of all the positive things you can create by helping just one person lead a better life. A simple act of kindness can change the world."

—Matilda Cuomo

Here are some volunteer ideas for retirement that offer unique opportunities for giving back and making a difference:

- **Art Therapy Volunteer**: Assist art therapists in facilitating creative workshops for individuals with mental health challenges or disabilities using art as a means of expression and healing.
- **Pet Hospice Volunteer**: Provide companionship and support to pets in hospice care, offering comfort, walks, and cuddles to animals in their final days.
- **Music Therapy Volunteer**: Volunteer with music therapists to bring the healing power of music to hospitals, nursing homes, or rehabilitation centers by playing instruments or singing for patients.
- **Backyard Bird Monitor**: Participate in citizen science programs by monitoring and documenting bird populations in your local area, contributing valuable data to ornithological research.
- **Home Energy Auditor**: Volunteer with organizations that provide free home energy audits to low-income families, helping them identify energy-saving opportunities and reduce their utility bills.
- **Recreational Therapy Assistant**: Assist recreational therapists in organizing and leading therapeutic recreational activities for individuals with disabilities or special needs, such as adaptive sports, arts and crafts, or outdoor adventures.

- **Historic Cemetery Preservation**: Volunteer with cemetery preservation groups to help restore and maintain historic graveyards by cleaning headstones, repairing fences, and documenting grave markers.
- **Food Recovery Volunteer**: Partner with food recovery organizations to collect surplus food from local businesses and redistribute it to food banks, shelters, or community meal programs, reducing food waste and fighting hunger.
- **Museum Exhibit Builder**: Volunteer at museums or historical societies to help design and build interactive exhibits, dioramas, or displays that engage visitors and bring history to life.
- **Storytelling Volunteer**: Share your storytelling skills with children in schools, libraries, or after-school programs, captivating young audiences with tales from different cultures or historical periods.
- **Seed Library Coordinator**: Help manage a community seed library by organizing seed swaps, workshops, and educational events to promote seed saving, biodiversity, and sustainable gardening practices.
- **Rural Library Bookmobile Driver**: Volunteer to drive a mobile library or bookmobile to rural communities, bringing books, educational resources, and literacy programs to underserved areas.
- **Library Volunteer**: Assist at local libraries by shelving books, helping with children's programs, organizing events, or teaching computer skills to patrons.
- **Beekeeping Educator**: Volunteer with beekeeping associations or environmental organizations to educate the public about the importance of pollinators and sustainable beekeeping practices.
- **Wildlife Habitat Restoration**: Assist conservation organizations in restoring and maintaining natural habitats for wildlife by participating in activities such as tree planting, invasive species removal, and habitat monitoring.
- **Aquaponics Gardener**: Volunteer with urban agriculture projects or community gardens that use aquaponics systems

to grow food sustainably, combining fish farming with hydroponic vegetable cultivation.

- **Disaster Preparedness Trainer**: Volunteer as a disaster preparedness trainer and teach community members how to create emergency plans, assemble disaster kits, and respond effectively to natural or man-made disasters.
- **Disaster Relief Volunteer**: Volunteer with disaster response organizations to provide aid and support to communities affected by natural disasters, such as hurricanes, floods, or wildfires.
- **Toy Repair Specialist**: Volunteer at toy repair clinics or repair cafes, and use your skills to fix broken toys and electronics and divert them from landfills.
- **Interfaith Dialogue Facilitator**: Volunteer with interfaith organizations to promote understanding and dialogue among people with different religious and cultural backgrounds. Facilitate discussions, events, and community projects.
- **Prison Hospice Volunteer**: Provide compassionate care and support to terminally ill inmates in prison hospice programs by offering companionship, listening, and comfort during their final days.
- **Graffiti Removal Crew**: Join community clean-up efforts to remove graffiti from public spaces, beautifying neighborhoods and discouraging vandalism through community pride and action.

Here are some additional volunteer ideas that cover a range of interests and causes:

- **Tutoring**: Offer your expertise and assistance as a tutor or mentor for children or adults who need extra support with academic subjects, literacy, or English language learning.
- **Animal Shelter Volunteer**: Assist at an animal shelter by walking dogs, socializing cats, cleaning cages, or helping with adoption events.
- **Meals on Wheels Driver**: Deliver meals to homebound seniors or individuals with disabilities who are unable to cook or shop for themselves.

- **Hospital/Nursing Home/Hospice Care Volunteer**: Provide assistance and comfort to patients, families, staff, and visitors by running errands or helping with administrative tasks in hospitals, nursing homes, or hospice care facilities.
- **Community Garden Organizer**: Help organize and maintain community gardens, which promote access to fresh produce and foster community engagement.
- **Environmental Conservation**: Participate in conservation projects such as tree planting, trail maintenance, or wildlife monitoring.
- **Environmental Cleanup**: Participate in beach cleanups, park beautification projects, or litter removal efforts to keep public spaces clean and safe.
- **Environmental Education**: Volunteer with environmental education programs, teaching children and adults about conservation, sustainability, and environmental stewardship.
- **Senior Center Activities Coordinator**: Plan and organize activities, outings, workshops, or social events for seniors at local community centers, retirement communities, or retirement homes.
- **Mentoring**: Serve as a mentor or coach for young people, helping them set goals, build confidence, and develop life skills.
- **Home Repair Volunteer**: Assist elderly or disabled homeowners with minor home repairs, maintenance tasks, or accessibility modifications.
- **Community Soup Kitchen or Food Bank Volunteer**: Volunteer at a community soup kitchen or food bank by sorting, packing, and distributing donations or preparing meals and serving them to the hungry.
- **Community Theater Volunteer**: Get involved with community theater productions by volunteering as an actor, stagehand, usher, or set builder.
- **Legal Aid Volunteer**: Provide pro bono legal assistance to low-income individuals or underserved communities through legal aid clinics or organizations.

- **Homeless Shelter Volunteer**: Assist at homeless shelters by serving meals, organizing donations, providing clothing, or offering support services to residents.
- **Habitat for Humanity Volunteer**: Help build or renovate affordable housing for families in need with Habitat for Humanity or similar organizations.
- **Crisis Hotline Volunteer**: Offer support and crisis intervention to individuals in distress by volunteering for a crisis hotline or helpline.
- **Arts and Crafts Workshops**: Lead or assist with arts and crafts workshops for children or adults in schools, community centers, or hospitals.
- **Foster Grandparent Program**: Participate in foster grandparent programs, providing mentoring, support, and companionship to children in schools or daycare centers.
- **Mentoring Programs**: Offer guidance and support to young people through mentoring programs in schools or community organizations.
- **Literacy Programs**: Assist adults in improving their literacy skills by tutoring or teaching reading and writing classes.
- **Arts and Culture Organizations**: Volunteer at museums, theaters, or art galleries by leading tours, assisting with exhibits, or participating in cultural events.
- **School Programs**: Assist teachers or school staff by tutoring students, organizing educational activities, or serving as a classroom aide.
- **Sports Coaching**: Volunteer as a coach or assistant coach for youth sports teams in your community.
- **Foster Grandparent Program**: Provide mentorship, support, and companionship to children in schools or daycare centers through foster grandparent programs.
- **Youth Mentorship Programs**: Join youth mentorship programs in schools, community centers, or youth organizations to provide guidance and support to young people.
- **Big Brothers Big Sisters**: Become a mentor with Big Brothers Big Sisters or a similar organization to build positive

relationships with children and help them reach their full potential.

- **Career Mentoring**: Share your knowledge and experience with job seekers or individuals looking to advance in their careers by offering career mentoring or coaching services.
- **Entrepreneurship Mentorship**: Mentor aspiring entrepreneurs or small business owners by providing advice, guidance, and support as they navigate the challenges of starting and growing a business.
- **Veteran Mentorship Programs**: Volunteer with veteran mentorship programs to support and assist transitioning service members as they reintegrate into civilian life.
- **Women's Mentorship Networks**: Join women's mentorship networks or organizations that empower and support women through mentorship, networking, and professional development opportunities.
- **Minority Mentorship Programs**: Participate in minority mentorship programs aimed at providing mentorship and support to individuals from underrepresented or marginalized communities.
- **STEM Mentorship**: Volunteer as a mentor in STEM (Science, Technology, Engineering, and Mathematics) programs to inspire and support students pursuing careers in these fields.
- **Arts Mentorship**: Share your passion for the arts by mentoring aspiring artists, musicians, writers, or performers and helping them develop their creative talents.
- **Leadership Development**: Mentor emerging leaders or aspiring managers by providing guidance, coaching, and mentorship to help them develop their leadership skills.
- **Community Service Mentorship**: Mentor individuals interested in community service or volunteerism by helping them identify opportunities, develop skills, and make a positive impact in their communities.
- **Financial Literacy Mentorship**: Volunteer as a mentor in financial literacy programs to help individuals learn about budgeting, saving, investing, and managing their finances responsibly.

- **Parenting Mentorship**: Offer support and guidance to new parents or parents facing challenges by serving as a parenting mentor and sharing your wisdom and experience.
- **Health and Wellness Coaching**: Mentor individuals interested in improving their health and wellness by providing guidance, encouragement, and support to help them achieve their goals.
- **Educational Advocacy Mentor**: Help students or parents with navigating the education system, advocating for their needs, and accessing resources and support services.
- **Elderly Mentorship**: Offer companionship, guidance, and support to older adults by serving as a mentor and providing socialization, assistance, and encouragement.
- **International Mentorship Programs**: Participate in international mentorship programs that connect mentors with individuals in other countries to share knowledge, skills, and cultural experiences.
- **Life Skills Mentorship**: Mentor individuals in developing essential life skills such as communication, problem-solving, decision-making, and time management.
- **Environmental Mentorship**: Mentor individuals interested in environmental conservation and sustainability by sharing your knowledge and passion for protecting the planet and promoting eco-friendly practices.

These mentoring opportunities offer meaningful ways to share your expertise, make a positive impact, and enrich the lives of others. Whether you're interested in education, career development, community service, or personal growth, there's a mentorship opportunity out there that's perfect for you.

Chapter 12

Civic Service

"To me, the function of politics is to make possible the desirable."

—Indira Gandhi

Would you like to become more involved in civic affairs? Here are just a few ways you can make a difference in your community and beyond. Whether you choose to volunteer, donate, advocate, or run for office, there are many opportunities to engage in political action and work toward positive change. (Admittedly, this section may be a bit more directed toward the U.S.A.)

- **Voting**: Exercise your right to vote in local, state, and national elections. Research candidates and issues to make informed decisions at the ballot box.
- **Campaign Volunteering**: Volunteer for political campaigns by making phone calls, canvassing neighborhoods, or assisting with event planning and coordination.
- **Political Donations**: Contribute financially to political candidates, parties, or causes that align with your values and priorities.
- **Community Organizing**: Get involved in community organizing efforts focused on issues such as education, healthcare, housing, or environmental conservation.
- **Letter Writing**: Write letters to elected officials expressing your opinions, concerns, and support for specific policies or legislation.
- **Petition Signing**: Sign petitions advocating for change on issues you care about, and encourage others to do the same.
- **Public Health**: Advocate for better public health policies. For example, in the U.S., there is a growing movement to re-evaluate the health benefits versus the health risks of

fluoridated public water supplies and whether the government is allowed to medicate the population via their public water source. This same water source makes its way into bottled beverages, canned soups, and other common grocery items, making it difficult for citizens to opt out if they decide they would rather not ingest this compound.

- **Attend Town Hall Meetings**: Attend town hall meetings, public forums, or legislative sessions to voice your opinions and engage with elected officials.
- **Join Political Organizations**: Join political parties, advocacy groups, or grassroots organizations working on causes you're passionate about.
- **Social Media Activism**: Use social media platforms to share information, raise awareness, and mobilize support for political campaigns and initiatives.
- **Political Education**: Educate yourself about political issues, government processes, and current events through reading, research, and attending educational events.
- **Protest and Demonstrate**: Participate in peaceful protests, marches, or demonstrations to advocate for change and raise awareness about important issues.
- **Run for Office**: Consider running for political office at the local, state, or national level to represent your community and enact positive change.
- **Serve on Boards and Commissions**: Volunteer to serve on local government boards, commissions, or advisory committees to influence policy decisions and address community needs.
- **Advocacy Work**: Engage in advocacy work by lobbying elected officials, drafting policy proposals, or organizing grassroots campaigns.
- **Legal Advocacy**: Support legal advocacy organizations working to defend civil rights, promote social justice, and protect vulnerable populations.
- **Political Journalism**: Write articles, blog posts, or opinion pieces on political issues and current events to inform and engage the public.

- **Political Art and Culture**: Create political art, music, theater, or literature that addresses social and political themes and sparks dialogue and reflection.
- **Political Book Clubs**: Join or start a political book club to discuss and debate books on political theory, history, or current affairs.
- **International Advocacy**: Get involved in international advocacy efforts by supporting human rights organizations, global health initiatives, or environmental conservation projects.
- **Civic Engagement**: Participate in civic activities such as volunteering, community service, or neighborhood cleanup efforts to contribute to the well-being of your community.

Conclusion

I really want you to be happy in retirement. You may have received this book as a gift or bought it for yourself, but either way I hope the ideas, stories, and suggestions in these pages stimulate your imagination for what this new frontier of your life can become. I've had friends who returned to their old job for a while, either because they were bored or pressured by their employer. I doubt that truly made them happy. For some people, the sudden, jarring break in the routine they followed for so many years is a tough adjustment.

I had a very rewarding career in the tech industry. In my job, I helped a lot of people solve a lot of very bad problems, and I got a lot of thank yous. It was one of those lucky jobs where you could actually see the benefit from what you contributed and often felt appreciated. And for the last 20 years of that job, I was able to work from home. I would get up 20 minutes before starting work, take a shower, and go to work in my pajamas. Pretty great. However, it also had a lot of stress, because, of course, these people were dealing with bad problems.

A few weeks after my retirement, I saw a notification in LinkedIn about a short video my former employer released. I decided to take a look. It was a kickoff for employee appreciation week. It was a presentation by the big guy expressing his gratitude for the hard work everyone puts in. It made me so nervous watching that video. It was simply an appreciation video, and it made me very tense. How crazy is that? Witnessing my own reaction further solidified how ecstatic I am to finally be released from that responsibility.

I hope you feel just as exhilarated to launch out into something new free from the shackles of your former responsibilities. There is no need to look over your shoulder. There is nothing for you back there. You have a fresh start.

Take some time to decide where you want to be. Perhaps the first thing you want to do is move to a different geographic location. Now is a great time to make that a reality.

I have one friend where he and his wife decided they didn't want to live anywhere. They sold their house, put a few possessions in a storage unit, and now live on the road hauling an RV behind their truck. They love to travel and see the country from the road. It is a lifestyle that makes them happy.

Take a break and decide what you want to do with your time. Embrace your freedom and reflect on what will make fulfill you as you look ahead. I wish you all the best.

Thank You!

I appreciate you purchasing my book. I know there are lots of options, and you went with mine.

I appreciate and value your time. I hope I gave you value for your time with this book, and I hope you feel others in or near retirement would benefit from this information.

Please consider adding a review on this platform.

It helps other readers, and it is a great way to support me as a small, independent author.

Your feedback helps me continue writing books that provide the results you are looking for.

—Joseph Hufschmitt

Here is a QR code link to the review page on Amazon.com (U.S. site).

Made in the USA
Monee, IL
12 August 2024

63713666R00100